Echoes of the Hurrians

Books by Theresa Vigil Hooper

Reglamento Provincial: California's First Book (1834)
Translated from the Spanish

Echoes of the Hurrians

Tracing an Ancient People from
the Caucasus Mountains to
Celt-Iberia to
the Spanish New World

By

Theresa Vigil Hooper

Edited by ML Brei
Cover Design by Theresa Vigil Hooper

Figures 1, 2, 5, 7, 8, 9, and 10 and Maps 1, 3, 5, 7, and 9 originally appeared on the world-wide internet. They are republished here under a Creative Commons license. Full attribution is listed under References.

Maps 2a and 2b are republished here with permission from the New Mexico Genealogical Society.

Second Edition
March 2025
ISBN 978-1-960808-06-6

Printed in the United States of America

Font: Baskerville 11 pt

In Memoriam to

The author's parents:
Joseph Vincent Vigil
Irene Aragon

Second father:
Benito Aragon

Half-brother:
Epimenio Aragon

Grandparents:
Abel Vigil & Ana Feliz Montoya
Celso Chavez Aragon & Leonides Zenaida Tafoya

Maternal Great Grandparents:
Theresa Valentina Santistevan Tafoya
& Epigmenio Leon Tafoya

Beloved aunt:
Clorinda Aragon (sister of Irene Aragon)

Beloved uncle:
Estanislado Vigil (brother of Joseph Vigil)

Dedicated to

Stanley Prescott Hooper
(1963-1986)

Youngest son of the author

✝

Contents

Introduction

The two monographs in this book present compelling research that connects an ancient people who existed over four thousand years ago in the southern foothills of the Caucasian Mountains to those who settled the Kingdom of New Mexico on the North American continent in the sixteenth century, A.D. The author establishes a path starting with the ancient Hurrians, progressing to people who migrated to the Celt-Iberian Peninsula and eventually arriving at the Kingdom of New Mexico.

The first monograph discusses the founding of The Kingdom of New Mexico, which we know today as New Mexico, the 47th state of the USA, and provides a brief history of the original migration of its European settlers. The second monograph jumps back in time to attempt to trace the path of our ancient ancestors starting at the sixth millennium BC and progressing to the ninth century AD.

+ + + + + +

The author's family was part of a small enclave of Spanish families who for over four hundred years persevered in building a life in a harsh landscape.

These Spanish families trace their lineage directly back to 1598 when the *First Families of New Mexico* (Primeras Familias) established a colonial settlement in the remote areas north of New Spain. The original pioneers and settlers are documented in the seminal work, *Origins of New Mexico Families* by Fray Angelico Chavez, first published in 1954.

Under the leadership of Don Juan de Oñate, a group of soldiers, families, and Franciscan priests left their homes in New Spain, the former seat of power of the Aztecs. They marched northward under two flags, that of the Spanish Crown (King Phillip II), and of the Catholic Church.

After traversing difficult terrain for almost 1500 miles, they stopped at the confluence of the Rio Grande and Rio Chama and established San Juan, the first capital of this kingdom. The frontier landscape soon proved to be harsh. Of the more than two-hundred names on the original Oñate lists, less than forty families established themselves permanently in the new lands.

The First Families of New Mexico are largely well-documented direct descendants of both the original conquistadors who arrived with Hernan Cortés in 1519 in the Yucatan Peninsula and settlers who arrived afterwards. The conquistadors and colonists of New Spain, for the most part, originated in Spain in the Celt-Iberian Peninsula under the rule of King Charles I (Charles V, Holy Roman Emperor, grandson of Queen Isabella and King Ferdinand).

After years of research, the author found not only the origins of her ancestors in Spain, but also where many of those ancestors may have originated as is discussed in the second monograph of this volume, ***The Origin of the Iberians***.

The ancient ancestors of the author's 15th century Spanish people, as far as can be ascertained, were a combination of descendants of the Tarshish, Phoenicians, Celts, Basques, Romans, Sephardic Jews, Visigoths, and to a surprisingly large degree a group of people who originated in the foothills of the Georgian Caucasus mountains. It is this latter group that can be shown to have had a tremendous impact on the character and nature of the author's Spanish ancestors.

Throughout its history the eastern region of the Caucasus has had many different names. The ancient Greeks called it Iberia, a Hellenized moniker that persisted. The land is referenced in classical treatises as the Kingdom of Iberia, Eastern Iberia, or Georgian Iberia. The people have been referred to as Iberians.

References in ancient manuscripts in Georgia indicate that a group of Caucasus Iberians migrated far to the west and settled in a region they called Western Iberia (which today is known as the Celt-Iberian Peninsula). The Caucasus Iberians referred to those settlers as their *Western Iberian brethren*.

As detailed in the second monograph, the people of Caucasus Iberia have a complicated identity, rendered obscure by the lack of available documented histories. There is linguistic and archeological evidence which strongly suggest, however, that they may have been descendants of the ancient Hurrians, who are also almost completely lost to history. We call the ancient people, the Hurrians, because of evidence that they spoke a language known as Hurrian. As of 2021, scholars have not determined what these people called themselves. For the purposes of this study, they will be referred to as the Hurrians.

To learn more about the nature and migrations of the Hurrian people, the author delved into ancient history and the documented migrations of people as recorded in the Old Testament.

This fascinating original research gives us insight about the nature of our First Families of New Mexico as has been nurtured and carried down in the familial genes for thousands of years. Knowledge of our ancient ancestors and the patterns of their lives help explain how our 16th century ancestors summoned the courage to venture forth into exceptionally remote and harsh territory to establish a new homeland.

In a recent turn of events, which the author was just beginning to explore, DNA studies support many of the assertions made in the second monograph. In particular, the migration of Iberian Caucasians from the foothills of the Georgian Mountains to the Celt-Iberian Peninsula has been definitively established and has been determined to have left an important and indelible impression on the genetic pool of the Celt-Iberian population.

These monographs are written from the perspective of the author: an American woman of Spanish descent, who was born and raised in a unique culture in Valencia, New Mexico, who lived for sixty years on the East Coast of America, and who was fully at home with all of the diverse peoples of the United States of America.

ML Brei, editor
Williamsburg, Virginia, March 2024

Monograph I

A Brief History of the Kingdom of New Mexico

(Now known as the states of New Mexico, Arizona, parts of Nevada, Colorado, and Texas of the United States of America)

2009

Figure 1.

Equestrian statue of Juan De Oñate. Oñate Monument
Center; Alcalde, NM. (Wikipedia Commons, 2011)

Oñate

On or about the year 1552 AD, Don Juan de Oñate was born in New Spain[1]. He married Doña Isabela de Tolosa in the year 1587. She was the granddaughter of Hernan Cortés, Conqueror of Mexico and the great-granddaughter of Emperor Moctezuma, Ruler of the Aztec Empire until 1520.

1598 AD

In 1598, Don Juan de Oñate financed and led an expedition into the area that would henceforth be known as the Kingdom of New Mexico (El Reino de la Nueva Mejico). It was an expedition undertaken on behalf of the King of Spain for the purpose of colonizing the area north of the known limits of New Spain. (Map 1) The new land was expected to include the area from the border city of Juarez, northward to the area near the Taos Pueblo.[2] Eventually the Kingdom extended from California, across Arizona, and into parts of Nevada, Colorado and Texas[3]. (Map 3)

---

[1] Formerly known as Mexica or The Triple Alliance: Tenochca, Texcoco, and Tlacopan, and now known as the Republic of Mexico

[2] Chavez, 1992

[3] Burke, 1973, Chavez 1989

Map 1. The general route of the Oñate expedition: El Camino Real de Tierra Adentro (The Royal Road of the Interior Land). This route links Mexico City with the northernmost outpost following the Rio Grande. Present-day political borders are shown. (US National Park Service, 2021)

This wasn't a purely military expedition. It included about 130 soldiers, many with families. Oñate brought his only son, Cristobal, *el nino de tierna edad*, a boy of tender age. A group of Franciscan Friars and indigenous (Indian[4]) servants were also included. Many of the people who joined the expedition did so with the intent to settle the remote area with enough soldiers to protect them.

In the year 1600, about 80 additional soldiers arrived, again, some with their families.

Traveling for more than three months over 1200 miles of rugged mountainous terrain and great stretches of uninhabited plains and deserts, these people had to be tenacious to succeed.

They brought their most prized possessions: horses,[5] herds of sheep, goats, and cattle; wagons pulled by oxen, farm implements, kitchen utensils, and seeds and saplings to plant and raise for food. They also brought medicines and herbs including but not limited to the biblical *buckthorn* known in New Mexico as *cascara sagrada* and coriander, known in New Mexico as *cilantro*, two kinds of mint, *hierba buena* and *poleo*, as

---

[4] For historicity purposes, the term *Indian* is used to refer in general to the great varieties of peoples who were inhabiting the lands prior to the arrival of the Spaniards. No insult to the descendants of the indigenous Americans or to people from the continent of India is intended. The author uses this term solely for historical context.

[5] Since pre-Biblical times, horses have enabled people to travel great distances. This use of horses is an important cultural marker that serves to draw connections with ancient peoples. See Monograph II for more information about the ancient people who were thought to be the first to tame and disperse horses throughout the ancient world.

well as saffron, the costliest of spices, the Biblical *Karkon* of the Song of Solomon, known as *zazfran* in New Mexico.[6]

They brought crops native to Mexico including chile, cultivated-tobacco, varieties of beans, the tomato, and new varieties of corn (including *Cristolina de Chihuahua*).[7]

The women brought personal accessories for living including linens, pillows, clothes and jewelry.

The records show that many of colonists could read and write so they brought their knowledge of mining and the science of metallurgy inherited from their centuries-old ancestors.[8] They also brought expertise in developing irrigation systems.

In 1599, the colonists founded the capital San Gabriel de Yunque-Ouinge near San Juan Pueblo along the Rio Bravo del Norte (known as the Rio Grande today). This is the second European town built in the United States.[9] It became the seat of the local government with Juan de Oñata as the first governor.

Although they found the land along the banks of the river to be fertile and easily irrigated, the settlers nevertheless set out at once to create irrigation systems which included main

---

[6] Genders, 1972

[7] Simmons, 1991, p 67

[8] It is believed that this knowledge originated with the ancient Hurrians of the Caucasus Mountains. See Monograph II.

[9] St. Augustine, Florida, another Spanish city, founded on September 8, 1565, is the first European city established in the United States. (Lummis, 1925)

ditches and secondary canals to efficiently move the waters of the river to individual fields.[10]

Further, it should not be forgotten how important it was to the Spanish people and to the Spanish King to bring Christianity to this new world. As a testimony to this priority, the first and second churches constructed in the United States were built by Spaniards. The first, San Agustin de La Florida (now called Cathedral Basilica of St. Augustine) in 1565, and the second, San Juan Bautista Church in San Juan Pueblo, Kingdom of New Mexico in 1598.

In 1608, a small group of settlers led by Captain Juan Martinez de Montoya, established a small villa in an uninhabited, fertile area with plentiful wood and water at the foothills of the Sangre de Cristo Mountains (the southern end of the Rocky Mountain chain). They called this villa *Santa Fe* (The Villa of Holy Faith).

Despite all of the preparations to establish themselves, the land and circumstances proved harsh towards settlement. By 1607, the people were struggling. Don Juan Oñate sent a letter of resignation to the Viceroy of New Spain, seeking help from the crown. The Viceroy of New Spain had difficulty finding a successor, somebody with the financial means and the military experience who would settle in that region.

---

[10] These irrigation measures proved critical during the dry cycles which followed the wet cycles. Two seasons of drought was enough to produce a famine. Over the years, as each new town was founded along the Rio Grande, irrigation systems were constructed sometimes before even the church was built. (Simmons, 1991)

At last in 1609, Pedro de Peralta, newly arrived in New Spain, was appointed Governor of the Kingdom. He reached New Mexico later that year and relieved Oñate as governor. Oñate returned to New Spain, and Peralta commenced to move the capital from San Gabriel to Santa Fe, building it from the ground up. He created a town council, established districts and farmlands around the town, dug canals as sources of water, and awarded land grants.

In 1610, construction of the Plaza Mayor (town square), and what is today known as the Palace of the Governors began. The Palace of the Governors is the oldest public building in continuous use in the United States today.[11]

Of more than 200 names found on the Oñate Lists, less than 40 established themselves permanently in the new land.[12] [13]

1680 AD

For the next 223 years the Kingdom of New Mexico was under the dominion of the King of Spain. Consequently, governmental aid and resources were too distant to be of pragmatic help. Communication was both difficult and

---

[11] Kelly, 2007, p 146

[12] Chavez, 1992

[13] Of the approximately 40 family names, at least 27 are ancestors of the author: Archuleta, Baca, Bernal, Cadimo, Carvajal, Durán y Chaves, de la Cruz, Gonzalez, Griego, Hinojos, Holguin, Jorge, Lopez de Ocanto, de Lluna, Marquez, Martin Serrano, Montoya, Perez de Bustillo, Ramírez, de Salazar, Robledo, Romero, Sanchez de Monroy, Torres, Valencia, Varela, Vazquez, Zaldivar. (Espinoza and Jaramillo)

limited. The colonists endured untold sacrifices both of loss of life and loss of fortunes, privations and struggles during those centuries.[14]

Reports to the King and church officials suggested that the land was no better than the "Miserable Kingdom" of Biblical times in Spain. Throughout the 1600's, droughts, Indian raids on both Indian pueblos and Spanish settlements, and illnesses resulted in severe hardships for the inhabitants of New Mexico.[15] They remained almost completely isolated from their brethren in New Spain. Their chief reliable influx of goods and information was delivered from Mexico via oxcart train, initially every three years.[16]

Yet, slowly, inexorably, more people arrived, and the descendants of the first colonists multiplied and survived. Over the centuries others would come from Greece, Italy, France, the Netherlands, Portugal, and Spain. Those who weren't hardy returned to less demanding lives in Spain, New Spain or other countries of origin.

The Pueblo Revolt of 1680

Although the Spanish colonists relied greatly upon the Pueblo peoples, the colonists lived in constant peril of attacks from the nomadic tribes.[17] The ever-present danger of

---

[14] Esquivel, 1999

[15] Burke, 1973, p 129

[16] Chavez, 1954

[17] Ibid.

Indian attacks reached a climatic moment in August, 1680, when a San Juan Pueblo Indian and a diverse force including nomadic tribes led a coordinated surprise attack against settlers living in northern outlying territories and the Rio Abajo (lower river) territories. Such an attack by the sedentary and typically peaceful Pueblo people was highly unusual.

A massacre of settlers, their household members and Franciscans ensued. Most survivors escaped to Santa Fe where they sought refuge within the walls of the Palace of the Governors. There, they were promptly held under siege by the Indian attackers.

The Spanish trapped in the Palace soon ran out of water and provisions. They escaped from the Palace and managed to retreat southward. Those who didn't make it to the Palace but nonetheless survived, joined their allies the Piro (from the pueblos of Alamillo, Senecu and Socorro) and the Tiwas (from Isleta) and retreated southwards as well.[18]

Those who survived took whatever possessions that they could and left everything else behind. Subsequently, the Pueblo revolutionaries destroyed everything that was Spanish.[19] Miraculously, an old wooden statue of Our Lady, known then as Our Lady of the Assumption, was rescued

---

[18] Jenkins, 1974, p 22

[19] Consequently, the material culture of the Spanish in New Mexico prior to the Pueblo Revolt is scant. Many of the churches and other buildings were burnt. Only religious metals, jewelry, and pieces of ceramics have been found by archeologists. Needless to say, no large wooden objects such as Spanish-colonial furniture survived this period. Most paper and cloth items were similarly destroyed. Only items that were worth hand-carrying had a chance of survival. (Kelly, 2007, p 160)

from a burning church and brought to safety in New Spain. (Figures 11 & 12)

Prior to the Pueblo Revolt of 1680, there were approximately 2500 Spanish colonists living in New Mexico. During the Revolt, it has been estimated that as many as 1000 Spaniards, including women and children were massacred by the Pueblo Indians.[20]

For the next twelve years, various Pueblo leaders assumed control of the Palace of the Governors, and attempted to rule over the diverse groups of Pueblo and nomadic tribes. They could not establish unity, and the Pueblo peoples suffered as a result. Historic enemies of the Pueblos, most notably the Apaches, who had initially joined in the revolt, proved once again to be dangerous enemies to the Pueblo tribes.

1692

The Reconquest

In 1688, Captain General Diego de Vargas Zapata Luján Ponce de León y Contreras, a marquis from Spain, was appointed Governor of New Mexico by royal edict.[21] In 1692, he led a small army of soldiers north along the Rio

---

[20] Burke, 1973, p 137

[21] Reeve, 1964, p 22

Grande and used diplomacy to secure the fealty of each Pueblo tribe as he and his soldiers passed through.[22]

By September, he was in control of both Santa Fe and the Palace of the Governors. This was accomplished without bloodshed. He and his men then marched north and "secured the submission of the northern pueblos ... and the complete pacification as far as the Hopi villages."[23]

Soldiers, colonists and Franciscans returned with him in 1693.[24] The Pueblo Indians who had been occupying the Palace of the Governor in Santa Fe were reluctant to relinquish their position and only did so after a battle with the Spanish soldiers that resulted in the loss of one life.[25] By 1696, peace had been secured. Our Lady of the Assumption was carried by General de Vargas, who gave it the new title La Conquistador.

---

[22] Jenkins, 1974, p 22

[23] Ibid. p 23

[24] His entourage included "100 soldiers, 70 families, a few single persons, and a number of servants; all told about 800 persons, including 17 Franciscan Friars." (Reeve, 1964, p 24)

[25] Reeve, 1964, p 24

Figure 2. Portrait of Captain General Diego de Vargas Zapata Luján Ponce de León y Contreras, by Julio Barrera, date unknown: collection of the Palace of the Governors, Santa Fe. (Wikipedia Commons, 2020) The original (1660s) is in the Capilla de la Cuadra de San Isidro, Madrid. Custody of Real Muy Ilustre y Primitiva Congregación de San Isidro de Naturales de Madrid. (Private Chapel) (Kelly, 2007, p 161)

17

Figure 11: Originally Our Lady of the Assumption. From Spain, carved of willow and European Olive wood during the early Renaissance. Brought to Santa Fe in 1625; was rescued from a burning church during the 1680 Pueblo Revolt, was carried to safety in New Spain. In 1693, she returned to Santa Fe with Gen. Diego de Vargas who then gave her the title "La Conquistadora." Oldest known religious statue in the U.S. (Chavez, 1934, p 8)

Figure 12: Our Lady of Peace. The original statue was modified throughout the years. She was pared down to be fitted with clothes and a wig and and given movable arms to hold baby Jesus. Her features were softened. She is cared for by the Confraternity of La Conquistadora and is carried in processions on Feast Days. Today, she is also known as Our Lady of Peace. (Chávez, 1934, p 89)

1696

After the reconquest, New Mexico was once more the northernmost outpost of the Viceroyalty of New Spain.

Many surviving members of the original families of New Mexico returned. New settlers, however, added to the family names. During the late 1600's and 1700's a few Frenchmen arrived and married Spanish women.[26]

Franciscan friars returned and took it upon themselves to reestablish abandoned pueblos and repair and build churches.[27]

As the population grew, a formal land-grant system was established whereby the governor was authorized to grant land from the royal domain to individuals and heads of households. The system was designed to allow families to establish separate communities, some of which served as defensive outposts, and to distribute cultivatable land while simultaneously

---

[26] This is remarkable as by Spanish law, non-Spanish foreigners were forbidden to enter Spanish lands in the colonies. French and Anglo traders who attempted to enter these lands were routinely captured and imprisoned in Chihuahua.

[27] Jenkins, 1974, p 29

protecting the lands used and occupied by the sedentary Indian tribes as required in the strict law code known as the Recopilacion de Leyes de los Reynos de las Indias. This system was in place until the U.S. occupation in 1846.[28]

1700s

The 18th century in New Mexico was marked by continual unprovoked attacks by Apache, Navahos, Utes, and Comanche against the Pueblos and the Spanish settlements. Intra-tribal hostilities among these tribes were frequent as well, causing general mayhem, frequent dislocations, and many deaths of the colonists. Throughout the century, campaigns against these attackers and subsequent peace treaties were the norm.

Meanwhile, the colonists "worked at their three-fold industry of cultivating the soil, raising livestock, and trading."[29] The predominant livestock at this time were sheep, goats, cattle, and horses.

By the middle of the century, new trading opportunities arose.[30] The Comanches, Apaches, and

---

[28] Jenkins, 1974, p 23

[29] Reeve, 1964, p 31

[30] Local staples available for trade included corn, wheat, a few vegetables (including chile), melons, pinons (pine nuts), and tree fruits. They also traded knives, axes, hoes, wedges, picks, and bridles. (Reeve, 1964) Trade was often conducted on a barter system as money rarely circulated. This system was vulnerable to exploitation.

The Rio Grande, North

Map 2a: Villages along the Rio Grande, settled in the
1600s and 1700s. (NMGS, 1998)

The Rio Grande, South

Map 2b: Villages along the Rio Grande,
settled in the 1600s and 1700s. (NMGS, 1998)

Ute were now actively trading with the colonists and pueblos. These nomadic tribes brought goods such as buffalo, deer, and antelope skins from the Mississippi Valley. They were also known to raid southern lands for horses and mules to trade to each other and to the colonists.[31]

Trading was typically done at annual fairs, a common meeting ground for colonist and Indian, where business and festivities took place.

The limited opportunities for trade were not adequate for the general well-being of the colonists and pueblos. By the end of the century, the northern frontier of New Spain was still suffering:

> "Plagued by isolation, weakened by campaigns and restricted by trade barriers, New Mexico was in a deplorable condition when Mexico declared her independence from Spain in 1821."[32]

Due to the restrictions on trade imposed by the Spanish authorities, material goods, as well as contact with North American neighbors was limited.[33] However, despite those restrictions, the citizens of New Mexico since before the 1800's were aware of the benefits of trading with the United States, as well as of the advantages of sending their sons to schools of higher learning in St. Louis, New York, and other major cities in North America, rather than to the alternative, Durango.

---

[31] (Reeve, 1964, p 31)

[32] Jenkins, 1974, p 31

[33] Chavez, Espinosa and Waide, 1973

As an example of their interest in the fate of their North American neighbors, many served in the Spanish military forces during the American War for Independence against the British in the 1770s.[34]

1822

After Mexico fought the War of Independence against Spain in 1821, the people of New Mexico were cut off from direct communication with Spain.

New Mexico had not been involved in the revolution. In fact, it was 1822 before news of the event reached New Mexico.[35] [36]

Notwithstanding their lack of involvement in these events, the people of New Mexico would have been unwilling to imperil their connection to the Catholic Church hierarchy by severing relations with the church officials in Mexico City. In addition, it would have been inadvisable to sever commercial connections with Mexico City as well.[37] Therefore, an

---

[34] As the result of having at least three ancestors who served in the Spanish military against the British during the American War of Independence in the 1770s, the author and her descendants are entitled to membership in the SAR and the DAR organizations, on both her maternal and paternal lines (Alarid, Santistevan and Vigil).

[35] Most in New Mexico learned of the event when the flag at the Palace of the Governors was changed. (Chavez, 1954, p 115)

[36] Chaves, Espinosa, and Waid, 1973, p 107

[37] In 1821, The Santa Fe Trail was established. This vital trade route opened important markets for New Mexican goods.

agreement was reached that New Mexico would legally be known as a "Department" (i.e. the Department of New Mexico) within the structure of the Mexican government, but as a separate entity. Thus the flag of Mexico flew over the capital in Santa Fe for twenty-four years.

1824

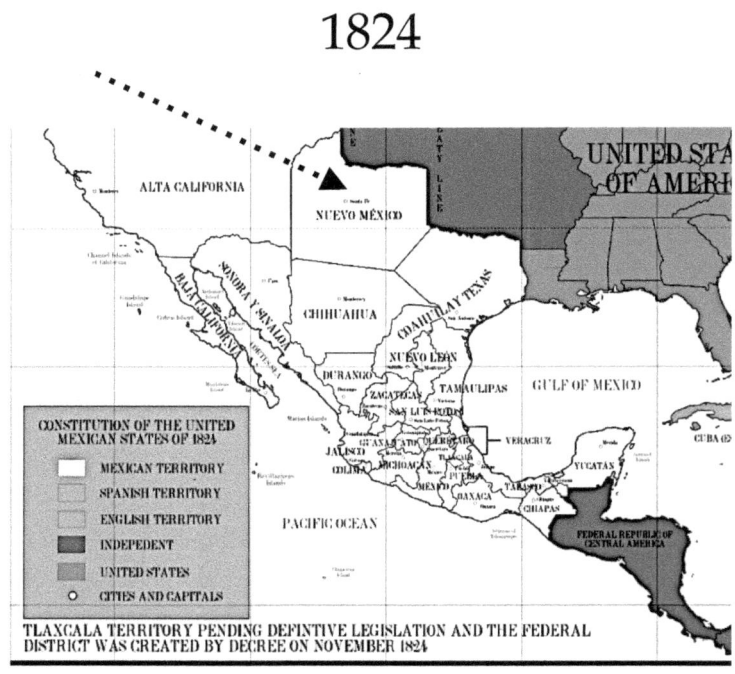

Map 3: 1824. The Department of New Mexico (dotted arrow) and other territories of the newly independent Mexican Republic (white region). (Wikipedia Commons, 2013)

During the twenty-four years of this administrative arrangement, when New Mexico was nominally under the jurisdiction of Mexico, less assistance was provided to the people of New Mexico by the Mexican government than had been provided by the Spanish King.

For instance, the local militiamen were responsible for fighting the nomadic Apaches and the Comanches, who regularly preyed on the Indian pueblos and on Spanish settlements. Mexico did not send aid.

It was only once, in later years, that a detachment of dragoons from Mexico was sent to New Mexico to fight the Texans.

Although legal and church documents were recorded in Mexico, New Mexico had its own system of government. Local militias were supported by local jurisdictions, and the Governors and government officials were people who were born and raised in New Mexico.[38] While the change in government meant little to the average person, it was this change in government which led to the increase in trade with the United States and opened the way for the people to profit from the expanded markets in the North.[39]

---

[38] The author is related to at least ten Governors of New Mexico who served terms beginning from the year 1822, through 1906. See Appendix.

[39] Chaves, Espinosa and Waid, 1973, p 107

Santa Fe in 1846, just before the Mexican-American War

1846

On August 18, 1846, Brigadier-General Stephen Watts Kearny (figure 3), commanding the United States Army of the West, invaded New Mexico and took over the government without firing a shot. In the words of General Kearny:

> "From the Mexican government you have never received protection. The Apaches and the Navajos come down from the mountains and carry away your sheep, and even your women, whenever they please. My government will correct all this. It will keep off the Indians, protect you in your persons and property; and, I repeat, will protect you in your religion…"[40]

New Mexico had no standing army, few weapons to fight a war, and no government funds to finance a defense against the United States Army.

Before Gen. Kearney's arrival, the sitting governor, Manuel Armijo, left Santa Fe accompanied by less than 100 dragoons. He had been informed that "men of prominence, such as Don Gregorio Vigil of the community of San Miguel"[41] and others, might not be willing to oppose the advancing army. Further, dissension among his officers and his men apparently convinced him of the futility of a struggle. The government in Mexico City was still

---

[40] Twitchell, 1923

[41] Ibid. pg 42

Gen. Stephen Watts Kearn

Figure 3. U.S. General Stephen Watts Kearny (Twitchell, 1923, p 5)

unorganized and in disarray as the various parties to the Revolution continued to fight among themselves. Governor Armijo did not expect, nor did he have reason to expect assistance from Mexico. Thus, Governor Armijo was "persuaded" to flee without a struggle.

Governor Armijo placed the government in Santa Fe in the hands of Lt. Governor, Don Juan Bautista Vigil y Alarid[42], who was left without a military force to protect the capital city of Santa Fe. He became the "de facto" Governor, and was the official who signed the agreement to turn over possession of the "Department" to the United States of America. In the words of Don Juan Bautista Vigil y Alarid:

> General: The address which you have just delivered, in which you announce that you have taken possession of this great country in the name of the United States of America, gives us some idea of the wonderful future that awaits us. …

> The inhabitants of this Department humbly and honorably present their loyalty and allegiance to the government of North America. No one in this world can successfully resist the power of him who is stronger. …

> Today we belong to a great and powerful nation. Its flag, with its stars and stripes, covers the horizon of New Mexico, and its brilliant light shall grow like a good seed well cultivated. We are cognizant of your kindness, of your courtesy and that of your accommodating officers and of the strict discipline of your troops; we know that we belong to the Republic

---

[42] son of Domingo Vigil and María Francisca Alarid. Born 1792, Sante Fe.

that owes its origin to the immortal Washington, whom all civilized nations admire and respect.[43]

With this, the reins of government were handed over and New Mexico became a Territory of the United States as of the year 1846.

General Kearny appointed Charles Bent as the first civil Governor of New Mexico and Donaciano Vigil as the first Territorial Secretary.[44] After the assassination of Governor Bent, Don Donaciano Vigil became Governor and served during the years 1847 and 1848.

In 1846 the people were given the choice of becoming citizens of the United States of America or of moving to Mexico. The people of New Mexico, a proud people who originally had lived in a Kingdom, (el Reino de la Nueva Mejico), gave up their titles (those who had them) and allegiance to the former New Spain to become U.S. citizens.

They henceforth considered themselves Hispanic (Hispano, Hispano-Americano), Spanish, Spanish-American or simply American. They did not then, (nor do they now), need to use labels, such as "Chicano", "Pachuco", "Latino", or others, imposed by outsiders, for themselves.

---

[43] Twitchell, 1923, p 31

[44] The three Vigil men mentioned are ancestors of the author.

Donaciano Vigil, early 1880s by Albright Art Parlors

b. 1802, Sante Fe. Son of Juan Cristóbal Vigil. Donaciano served as interim governor, territorial governor, and territorial secretary after Kearny's army took possession of New Mexico.

1848

In 1848, the United States and Mexico signed the Treaty of Guadalupe Hidalgo, which ended the conflict between Mexico and the United States. This treaty, as a formality, transferred legal jurisdiction of New Mexico to the United States. The actual transfer, of course, had already been accomplished as a result of the invasion of 1846.

Let it not be forgotten that Mexico had lost the war, nonetheless, under the terms of the Treaty, Mexico received $15,000,000 in return for having ceded New Mexico and California to the United States (see Map 5).

Figure 5. New Mexico Territory coat of arms, 1850. (Wikipedia commons, 2014)

Valencia County 1850

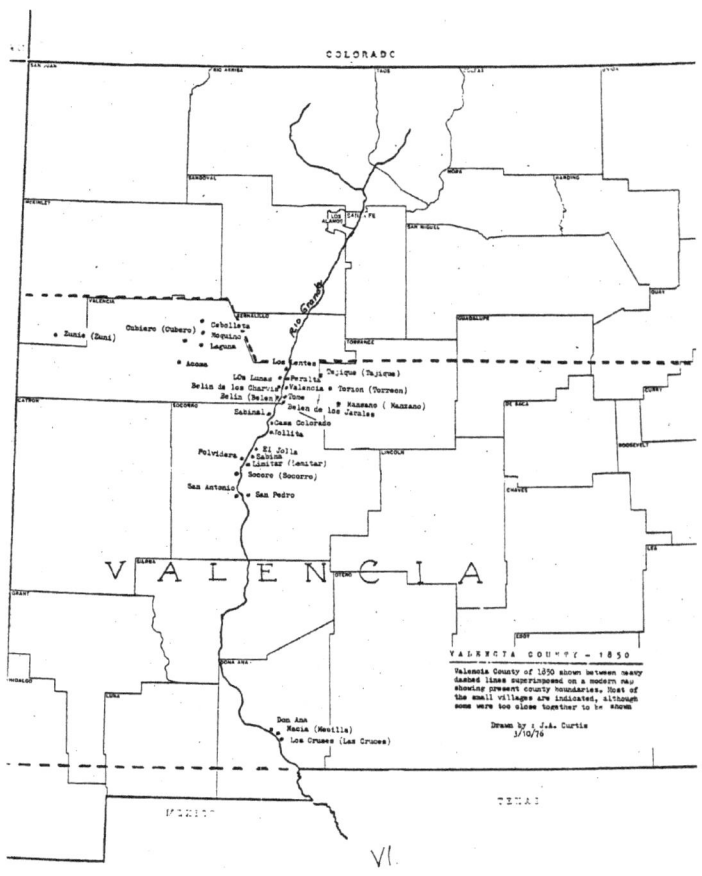

Map 4: The extent of Valencia County, 1850. Current political boundaries are shown. (Curtis, 1976)

NM Territory 1852

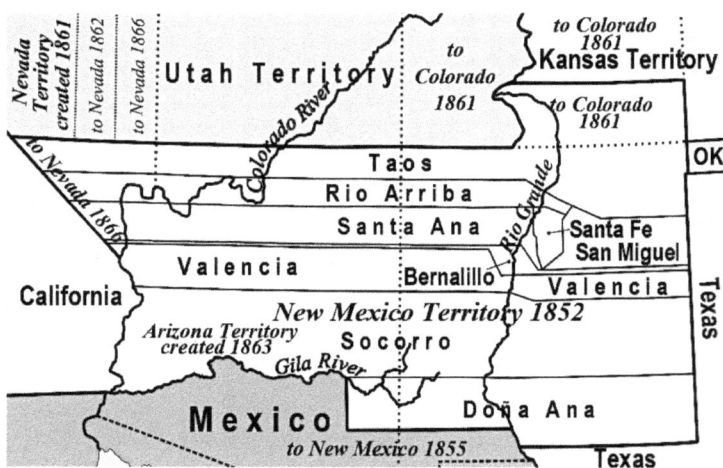

Map 5: 1852 New Mexico Territory formally transferred to the United States. Valencia County originally covered more than half of New Mexico. In 1850, Valencia County extended all the way across Arizona as far as California. By 1852, Valencia was further reduced. Dashed lines indicate present state boundaries. (Wikipedia Commons, 2017)

1912 and Beyond

In 1912, the Territory of New Mexico became the 47th state of the United States of America.

The political parties were divided regarding the advisability of becoming a state. The Democrats were against the change. The Republicans were in favor. In their wisdom, the people chose statehood and the Republicans prevailed.

It was a natural transition. The people of New Mexico had been United States citizens since 1846. More than 150 years earlier, after the 1696 Reconquest of New Mexico, those who had been there since 1598 already considered themselves Americans.[45]

---

[45] Burke, 1973, p. 157

Conclusion

This very small group of people, with an abiding faith, by their own initiative, hard work and perseverance, and frequently with only their personal possessions to sustain them, were able to survive the difficulties of moving to an often hostile land: an arid, frequently cold and windy and never very fertile land,[46] a completely different land from which they had come with their wives, children, and sometimes parents.

Although the majority of the people in this narrative are Hispanic, there are among them Italians, Portuguese, Germans, Jewish, French, Greek, and Flemish who have contributed to the person who is the author. Very much like the English, the Irish, the Germans, and all the other people who have come to this land from over the seas, including those early people who came across the Bering Sea, they came with their families, with the hope of a better life, and worked diligently to achieve that goal through all the obstacles, the hardships and the setbacks which they encountered, and which are almost impossible to imagine.

These few pages, with these very few names, attest to the fact that we and our latest generations are here today only because a small number of courageous and undaunted people came before us. This monograph is written as a tribute to them.

---

[46] Lummis, p. 91

Monograph II

The Origin of the Iberians

The Journey from the Caucasus
Mountains to the Sangre de Cristo
Mountains in Northern New Mexico

4000 BC to 1598 AD

Preface

Editor's Note: The Spaniards who arrived with Cortés in the early 16th century in the New World were a bold people who risked their lives to establish new lands for their king and faith.

We ask at this point, what was it in their background or even their genetic make-up that gave them the courage, the competence, and indeed the inspiration to pursue this audacious endeavor? And how did they summon the strength to remain loyal to the mission and persevere against overwhelming odds?

Who were these people, who hailed from the Celt-Iberian Peninsula?

We start by asking, why is the Celt-Iberian Peninsula called "Celt-Iberia?" We know that the Celtic people are present in western Europe ca. 2000 BC. By 600 BC they were a significant presence in central Spain. We are now learning through DNA analysis and archeological evidence that sometime around 2500 BC, another large group of people, mostly males, from the Eastern European Caucasus, traveled to the Peninsula and stayed. Their land of origin was known by the ancient Greeks as the Kingdom of Iberia. It's reasonable to conclude that the fusion of the Iberians and the Celts was thereby reflected in the name of their new homeland: the Celt-Iberian Peninsula.

The next question becomes: who were the ancient Eastern Iberians? In western scholarly circles, this subject has long been regarded as somewhat of an enigma.

This monograph hopes to connect the dots of the disparate knowledge that can be gleaned from traditional and new sources to answer this question. The ultimate goal is to shed light on the characteristics that have been passed down through the millennium and may be relevant today to the large number of us who are their distant descendants.

MLB, editor

The history of Georgian Iberia (or Eastern Iberia) and her people has yet to be uncovered in its entirety. There is little information available in the West regarding the people who first inhabited the foothills of the Caucasus Mountains perhaps as early as during the late Mesolithic and the early Neolithic periods, from 13,000 to 8000 BC.

In order to gather as much information as possible on their origins, a variety of sources have been consulted, including the latest archeological information. Inasmuch as this information is incomplete and scattered, it has also been necessary to rely on information which has been available for many years.

TVH, author

A Land Between Two Seas

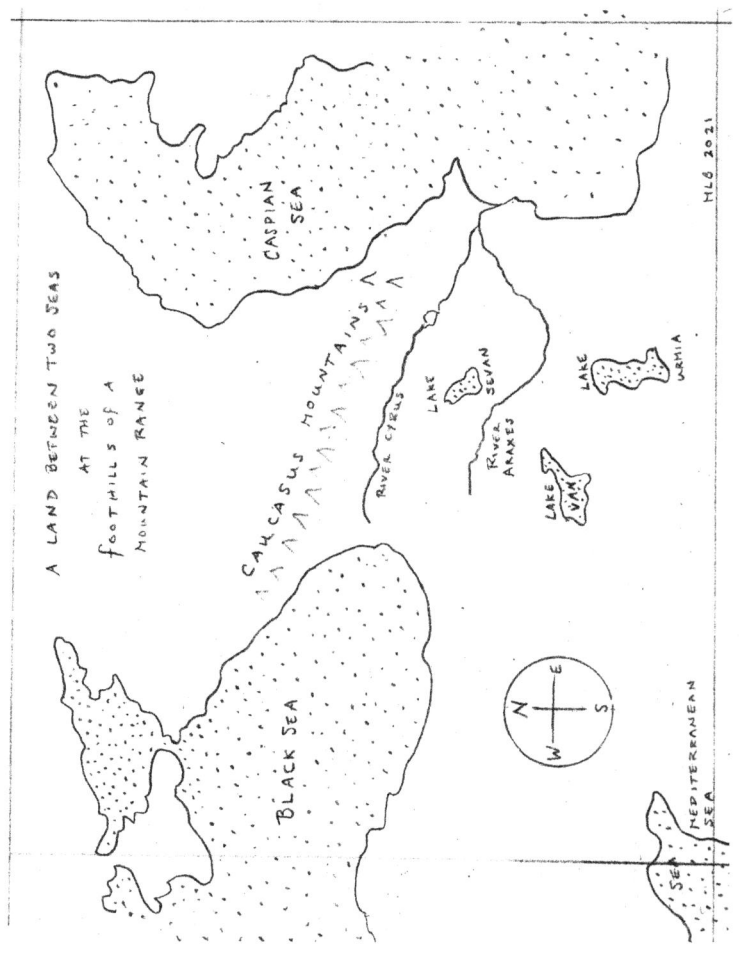

Map 6: The general area (using modern geographic names) south of the Caucasus mountain range, north of ancient Mesopotamia, east of ancient Anatolia, and east of the Mediterranean Sea. This is believed to be the land of the ancient Eastern Iberians and the homeland of an even older people known as the ancient Hurrians.

Overview

The Ancient Kingdom of Iberia is an eastern land which sits between two seas, between two rivers, among three lakes, and at the foothills of a famous and well-known mountain range.[47] (Map 6)

It is not a large country, but over time, it covered great expanses of territory, with a multitude of inhabitants. Early people of this land can be reasonably characterized as Neolithic[48] who as a consequence of discovering copper and developing the science of metallurgy prior to 3500 BC, can also be characterized as late Neolithic or Chalcolithic.

For unknown reasons, the land itself has been known by many names, not always Iberia, and its people have seldom been called Iberians. They have been known by many names, however, they have not always been known by the name of their homeland.

---

[47] Today, these features are known as the Black Sea and the Caspian Sea; Lake Van, Lake Sevan, and Lake Urmia; the Cyrus River (Kura River) and the Araxes River; and the foothills of the Caucasus Mountains.

[48] The Neolithic people are known for their use of stone tools intentionally shaped and/or polished. They depended on domesticated plants or animals, and had settled in permanent villages. They were associated with pottery and weaving.

This remains a mystery which may not be unraveled by the time the results of the research for this monograph have been exhausted.

The land itself, however, has been referred to as the "Land of the Hurrians"[49], although the name "Hurrian" has no geographic connotation.[50]

Thus to understand who the ancient Eastern Iberians were, another puzzle, the origin of the Hurrians, must be considered.

The Hurrians, as an ethnicity, have been identified as early as 5000-4000 BC through archeological excavations; by the Sumerians since at least 3200 BC; and through Biblical texts post Flood. The earliest extant written record of the Hurrians is from approximately 2300 BC.

Western knowledge regarding the origin of the Hurrians is scarce, yet archeologists have long believed that they, an isolated people, were drawn from the foothills of the Caucasus Mountains southward to take advantage of the more developed regions in northern ancient Mesopotamia. A on-going excavation of the ancient Hurrian city of Urkesh in Syria, however, provides evidence that the Hurrians were not simply "another wandering tribe in the fractious Middle East."[51] Indeed, they "may have been present [in Northern

---

[49] Buccellati, 2007

[50] Fournet 2010

[51] Lawler, 2008

Mesopotamia lands] 1000 years earlier [3000 BC], just as nearby Mesopotamians began to create the first cities."[52]

Archeological evidence supports the theory that Urkesh was an important urban center of the Hurrian civilization in ancient Syria and had strong ethnic ties with existing Hurrian population centers in the Caucasus foothills.[53] Thus, although it is accepted that the homeland of the Hurrians was originally in the foothills of the Caucasus,[54] their early appearance and influence in northern Mesopotamia suggests that they were the peoples who brought advanced technology to these southern lands and helped usher in the great civilizations that followed.

Linguistic evidence suggests that the Eastern Caucasian languages are offshoots of the Hurrian-Urartian group of languages. Therefore, a familial connection between the Iberians and the Hurrians appears to be indicated. The connection may be a later connection rather than a connection from the earlier periods.

As the research on the Iberians and their forefathers, the Hurrians, has progressed, it has become increasingly apparent to this author how extraordinary these people must have been.

They made important societal contributions to the lands they inhabited. They were known for their knowledge of metallurgy; they mined and traded copper, silver and tin as

---

[52] Ibid.

[53] Ibid.

[54] Buccellati, 2007

they moved southward. They knew how to design irrigation systems. They introduced horses and the chariot used by the great ancient civilizations (including Egypt), and they wrote treatises on how to train horses.

They established a set of laws that influenced both Semitic and non-Semitic groups. Their pantheon of gods and goddesses influenced the religions of neighboring peoples.[55] The oldest known example of written music (including the names of the Hurrian composers) are documented in Hurrian texts from Ugarit that date back to 1400 BC.

Although their name and the name of their homeland has changed constantly over thousands of years, the people have seemed to accept these changes, or perhaps, they have been compelled to accept them. Who these resilient, inventive and courageous people have been and where they are today remains to be determined.

---

[55] Carvings and statues of Hurrian gods and goddesses indicate their assimilation across the various cultures of the ancient Near East. Frequently the same deities are referred to by different names in different pantheons. For instance the Hurrian goddess Shaushka was identified with Ishtar of Nineveh. (Singer, 2016) See Figure 7a.

Shaushka

Figure 7a: One depiction of the Hurrian goddess Shaushka, *The Great One*, goddess of healing, love, marriage, war, etc. She is identified by her split skirt with display of one leg. Her symbol is the lion. Portable statues (in ivory or wood) of Shaushka attended pilgrimages and traveled between royal courts. The Armana Letters document the arrangements for her trip to Egypt by King Tushratta to bless Pharaoh Amenhotep III with healings and to show good faith. She was later returned to the Hurrian king. This is a detail of a bas-relief from Yazilikaya Sanctuary near ancient Hattusa. (Wikipedia Commons, Textier, 1862)

It is not known whether they have disappeared altogether. Yet we do know that they were well known seven thousand years ago and until the middle of the first century AD.

Cartographic and Geographical Considerations

To understand ancient Iberian history, it will be necessary to first describe the geography of the land.

The region was called Iberia by the Greeks during the sixth century BC. (Map 9) It has also been called Caucasia, Trans-Caucasia, the Land of the Hurri, the Kingdom of Mitanni, the Kingdom of Van, the Kingdom of Kartli, Ararat, Urartu, the Land of the Nairi, Colchis, Lazica, Pontus, Armenia, Georgia, and Azerbaijan. There is a full history associated with each of these names.

Immediately, we recognize the place name "Ararat", the mountain where Noah's ark is said to have reached land after the flood. This is an indication that knowledge of Biblical history is of value for this study.

Iberia is situated just south of the Caucasian Mountains between the Euxine Sea, now called the Black Sea, and the Caspian Sea. The earliest inhabitants appear to have first settled in an area between the Cyrus River now called the Kura River and the Araxes River, both just south of the Caucasus, and surround a lake called either Lake Gokha, Lake Erivan or Lake Sevan, and south as far as Lake Van. (See Map 6)

It appears that as early as the sixth millennium, these people migrated south and west as far as the Khabur River Valley. They were the Tell Halaf (6500 - 5500 BC) and the Tell Brak people, the potters who created the distinctive, high-quality, and widely distributed Halaf pottery[56], which dates from the sixth millennium BC.

This population also migrated south of Lake Van and east of the Tigris River as far as Kirkuk and past Lake Urmia which is now in Iran, and as far as the Zagros Mountains which are approximately two hundred miles south of Lake Urmia. There is no doubt that they occupied the land west of the headwaters of the Euphrates River as far as Carchemish and Aleppo, which are settlements near the border between Syria and Anatolia. Excavations at Carchemish have revealed that a late Neolithic or Chalcolithic culture existed at the site sometime ca. 3000 BC.

From what we know thus far, the narrow land area that was the homeland of the Hurrians, could not have sustained a large group of people. The land was very limited, between several bodies of water and a mighty mountain range, therefore it would not have been a suitable place for a large population. The people would have found themselves, very early in their history, with the necessity of moving to other lands. Further, the land was not readily accessible from the more heavily populated mainland of Anatolia and

---

[56] Halaf pottery: polychrome with geometric & animal designs; unpainted cooking ware; and pottery with burnished surfaces. Found in diverse parts of northern Mesopotamia: Nineveh, Tepe Gawra, Chagar Bazar, Tell Amarna, and places in Anatolia.

Mesopotamia, thus isolating them. However, with abundant water for fishing and land for farming and grazing at the foothills of the mountains, they would have been well nourished and sturdily built and resourceful in their isolation.

According to several sources, an unknown group of people occupied a broad area of fertile farmland stretching from the Khabur River Valley to the foothills of the Zagros Mountains since approximately 5000 BC. The Khabur River Valley had a central position in the metal trade in copper, silver and tin, which were found in the Anatolian Highlands as far north as the Caucasus.

Historical maps provide additional clues. During the times of the Persian Empire (521 BC) (Map 9), the reign of Alexandra the Great (320 BC) (Map 10), the age of the Seleucidian and Parthian Kingdoms (250 BC - 100 BC), this land was known as Iberia.

By 100 BC, however, Iberia is cut off from the coast of the Black Sea (this western area becomes Colchis) indicating that the earlier inhabitants lost some of their land.

Furthermore, maps of the Roman Empire do not include Iberia as previously known. By 800 AD, Iberia (located between the two seas and two rivers) is once again restored as a place name.

By 1200 AD, the area is no longer named Iberia. It is now called Georgia.

Biblical Ancestry

According to biblical history, the area between two seas, the Euxine Sea, now known as the Black Sea, and the Caspian Sea, was settled by Ashkenaz, a descendant of Noah, Japheth, and Gomer.

Gomer settled west and north of the Caucasus and on the eastern shores of the Euxine Sea.

Magog, another son of Japheth, settled north and east of the Caucasus and on the western shores of the Caspian Sea.

Therefore it was Ashkenaz who settled around Lake Gokecha or Sevan, one of the lakes in the heart of the land of the Iberians, the other lake was Lake Van. Ashkenaz is the ancestor of a group of Hebraic people known as the Ashkenazi.

Arpachshad, a grandson of Noah, the son of Shem, and the ancestor of Shelah and Eber, settled the area around Lake Urmia which is now in Iran, and is east of the Tigris River and southeast of Lake Van.

Therefore, it appears that two descendants of Noah - one a descendant of Shem and the ancestor of Shelah and Eber, and one a descendant of Japheth and Gomer settled very near to each other and possibly both contributed to the population of Ancient Iberia.

The Hurrians may have been the Horites of the Old Testament[57] who moved to Palestine via Haran (a Hurrian city) in Syria, to an area east of the Jordan River, and as far as Shechem, north of Jerusalem.[58]

The Hurrians were known to be closely related to the Proto-Arameans and the Assyrians. The Arameans were descendants of Noah and Shem. The Assyrians were descendants of Noah, Shem and Asshur whose empire existed from ca. 1900 BC to ca. 605 BC, in Mesopotamia. Their well- known city, Nineveh, was destroyed by the Medes and the Babylonians. The Medes were descendants of Noah and Japheth. According to biblical history, Nimrod, who was a descendant of Noah, Ham and Cush, built the cities of Babylonia, Akkad, Shinar and Nineveh.

---

57 Cartwright, 2018

58 This is not a settled point. Some argue that if the Horites were Semitic, they could not have been Hurrians, as Hurrians were clearly non-Semitic.

Chronology

To understand the spread of the ancient Hurrians and how they may have become the ancient Eastern Iberians, it is necessary to view the facts chronologically.

6000 to 5000 BC

Based on results of excavations at Tell Halaf[59] and Tell Brak at the upper Khabur Valley in Northern Mesopotamia, it appears that an advanced culture produced the Tell Halaf pottery.[60] This society is believed to have contributed to the development of the cities of the Ubaid period, ca. 6000 BC to 4000 BC, the Uruk period, 3000 BC, and to the successes of the early Sumerian period of 3200 to 3000 BC. There is no information regarding the name these people called themselves in the sixth millennium.

---

[59] Located on the headwaters of the Khābur River — modern-day northeast Syria

[60] Other items produced include amulets, stamp seals (geometric designs) and female terra-cotta figurines. (Met, 2003)

Based on results of excavations at Tell Mozan (the ancient city of Urkesh)[61] at the foothills of the Taurus Mountains, fifty miles north of Tell Brak, it is likely that Hurrians were established in the highlands to the north of Urkesh[62] as early as the mid-sixth millennium. These people might have been indigenous to the mountainous region.[63]

These excavations have revealed evidence of an on-going turn-over of various ancient peoples in this area over a 5000-year period.

4000 - 3000 BC

From pre- 4000 BC to ca. 3500 BC, considerable evidence points to a Calcolithic culture which existed before 3500 BC, when copper was discovered and copper metallurgy was developed in the regions of the Caucasus, Armenia, and Asia Minor. These people would have been the ancestors of the Iberians: the Hurri or *Hurrians*.

During the fourth millennium, the Hurrians "inhabited the the upper Habur and Tigris Rivers up to the Taurus and Zagro Mountains, especially around Lake Van."[64] For

---

[61] Modern day Syria. This excavation was halted in 2011 A.D. due to Syrian wars.

62 Urkesh is thought to have been a major Hurrian city, one of a small number of such cities located along the Piedmont of the Taurus range.

63 Buccellati, 2007, Frahm, 2019

64 Cartwright, 2018

centuries they mined the hills for copper, refined their use of it, and traded it. They eventually became merchants, travelers, and later warriors.

The aforementioned excavation at Urkesh has revealed a thriving society between 4000 and 3000 BC, with a well-established Hurrian population who had cultural and economic ties to the people in the northern highlands.[65]

The Hurrians expanded across upper Mesopotamia[66] from about ca. 3000 BC and continued to flourish.

As the Hurrians expanded into Syria, the local people adopted the Hurrian pantheon of gods and added them to their own pantheon.

From about 3200 BC, the Sumerians, whose capital was Ur,[67] developed a pictograph writing system which led to cuneiform writing on clay tablets. [68] [69]

---

65 Buccellati, 2007

66 As indicated in linguistic analysis.

67 Located in Mesopotamia between the Tigris and the Euphrates Rivers.

68 As a result, their early dynastic period saw the beginning of recorded history.

69 From early texts it is apparent that the Sumerians codified civil law and established efficient commercial and banking practices. Their belief system included a history of the world, a deluge, the search for eternal life, and life after death. Their frequent battles over water rights and border lines among the city states of Shinar led to their developing military equipment and organization, which was superior to that of the contemporary Egyptians.

The Hurrian language[70] being wholly distinct and unlike any other language, distinguishes the Hurrians from other ancient peoples. The Hurrians used the Sumerian cuneiform writing system as evidenced by clay tablets found in Urkesh. They also used the Ugaritic[71] cuneiform alphabetic script and the Hittite hieroglyphics.

From written texts that have been found, it appears that the Sumerians and other people used Hurrian words for copper terminology.

Copper was traded south to Mesopotamia from the Highlands of Anatolia. The Khabur River Valley was the center for the trade of copper, silver and tin. This is the same region thought to be populated by the Hurrians since the early 2000's BC until ca. 1275 BC when a people called the Mitanni disappeared. Subsequently the area was populated by the ancient Iberians. See 1700 BC section.

---

[70] Documentary evidence of the Hurrian language spans the years between 3000 BC and 1200 BC

[71] Ancient Ugrite was a port city on the Mediterranean coast in what is now North Syria. It was first settled ca 6500 BC.

Figure 7: Foundation tablet ca 2000 BC: Hurrian King Atalshen of Urkish and Nawar, Habur Bassin presents a dedication to Nergal, god of the netherworld. Louvre Museum AO 5678. (Wikipedia Commons, ALFGRN, 2006)

2600 - 2100 BC

Late Bronze Age

The modern site of Tell Brak was known as Nagar in ca. 2600 BC and was ruled by the Akkadians. Shortly thereafter, the Hurrians took control of the city and called it Nawar. (Map 7)

By 2500 BC the people of Central Asia were taming and training horses. The Hurrians are believed to have introduced the horse to the Near East since before 2000 BC. They were also known as horse trainers. Archeologists have found a manual on horse training, written during this time period, by a Hurrian named Kik-kull.

The name of an area called Ishuwa, a Hurrian word which means *horseland*, was populated by Hurrians. Ishuwa is thought to have been located in the Anatolian Highlands or Cilicia[72].

From the Bible we learn that King Solomon imported 12,000 horses from Cilicia. The area of Cilicia is believed to have been settled by Tarshish, a descendant of Noah, Japheth and Javan. Also according to Biblical history, Tarshish is identified with Tartessus   in southwestern Spain. Linguistically, the word Tartessus is the Aramaic form of the name Tarshish.

By 2500 BC until 2000 BC, the Egyptians traveled to Biblos in Phoenicia, now known as Lebanon, for Cedar of Lebanon logs. In Biblical history, the Phoenicians were the sea-faring descendants of Canaan who settled at Tyre and Sidon. Canaan was the descendant of Noah and Ham. A place name in the south of Spain known as Sidonia is known to have been settled by the Phoenicians, as was Gadir or Gades, as late as 1100 BC It is now known as Cadiz. The settlement

---

[72] A region in south central Asia Minor.

called Tartessus[73] is known to have been a Phoenician urban civilization in Southern Spain, the name of which denotes a center for smelting metallic ore.

In 2500 BC, a group of people migrated from the Caucasus region to Spain. After co-existing with the local peoples on this western peninsula, these eastern Europeans eventually became the dominant male presence in late Bronze Age Spain.[74] There is some indication that groups of eastern people continued to travel throughout the centuries on Phoenician vessels to reach Spain's shores.

By 2500 BC the Gilgemesh story was well-known throughout Babylonia and Assyria.
Hurrian texts dating to ca. 2300 BC were found in the Mardin region of eastern Anatolia.

Around 2000 BC, copper technology from Spain spread into western Europe and diffused widely, apparently with the Bell Beaker culture.[75]

---

[73] Is Tartessus in Southern Spain the region where Tarshish descendants landed after traveling in Phoenician vessels to settle in Spain? Did the people who discovered copper and developed copper metallurgy in Eastern Iberia ca. 3500 BC also travel to Spain before 2000 BC to mine and develop copper, or perhaps tin, needed to produce bronze, in Tartessus?

[74] Recent DNA analysis shows that most present-day men in Spain/Portugal can trace their paternal ancestry to this early group of eastern people. (Heritage, 2019)

[75] A group of late neolithic, early Bronze Age people ca. 2000 BC who migrated throughout Europe and into the British Isles. Known for the trail of distinctive bell-shaped pottery that they left throughout their migrations.

Middle East 2300 BC

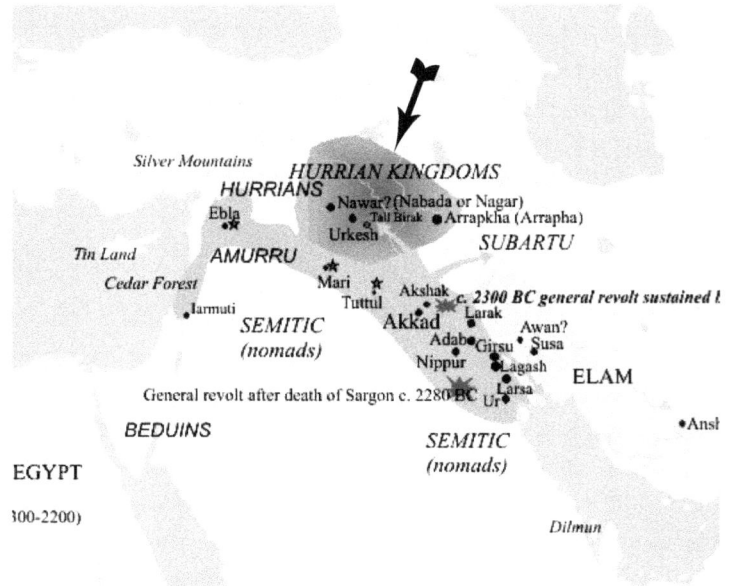

Map 7: Hurrian Kingdoms in the Middle East: ca. 2300 BC .
The two large bodies of water at the top of the map
represent the Black Sea and the Caspian Sea. The Caucasus
Mountains are between these two seas. The Hurrian
Kingdoms are in the sideways pear-shaped area north of
Mari. (Wikipedia Commons, by Jolle at Catalan, 2004)

2140 B. C.

Among the earliest of the monuments found at an excavation at ancient Ur was a brick with the following inscription which is of great interest. The inscription has been translated to read as follows:

> Beltis[76], his Lady, has caused Uruk, the pious Chief King of Hur, and King of the Land of Akkad, to build a temple to her.

The records show that King Urukh who was also known as Lig- Bagas, was "The greatest of Babylonian builders, except Nebuchadnezzar". King Urukh is known to have built the following temples:

> At Ur, to the Moon god.
> At Erech, to Ishtar,
> At Nipur, to Bal, and one to his consort Beltis,
> At Zurgal, to the King of the gods,
> Also a temple tower (ziggurat), and a palace at Ur.

His son, Dingi (or Shulgi) was a ruler of the Third Dynasty of the Empire of Ur, who ruled from 2140 to 2030 B. C., or from 2094 to 2047 B. C, and is considered by some to have been the single most influential ruler of the dynasty. Among

---

[76] May be identified as an Ishtar-like goddess.

other accomplishments, he built a temple at Babylonia. Was Urukh, the Chief King of Hur, a Hurrian?

Throughout the second millennium, Hurrian laws (as recorded on tablets found in ancient Nuzi[77]) were widely followed in upper Mesopotamia.[78]

BELL BEAKER POTTERY

Figure 8. Examples of Bell Beaker pottery at the Museum for Prehistory and Early History, the State Museum of Berlin. (Wikipedia Commons, Einsamer Schutze, 2011)

---

[77] Nuzi was an agricultural town: originally an Akkadian town called Gasur, today known as Yorghan Tepe, Iraq, southwest of modern Kirkuk, Iraq.

[78] Carroll, 1985, p 55-56

Hurrian Lion

Figure 9: Hurrian foundation peg depicting the forepart of a lion, ca 2200-2100 BC. From Urkesh. Inscribed: "Tishatal, king of Urkesh built a temple for the god Nergal [god of underworld], May the god Nubadag protect this temple. May Nubadag destroy whomsoever seeks to destroy [it]...." Placed under the temple. Copper alloy. Approx. 4x3x3 inches. (The Met)

Pre-1900 BC

According to Bible history, Abraham, a descendant of Noah, Shem and Eber, was born in Ur. He moved from Ur with his family to Haran[79], north of Ur in Mesopotamia, where they lived in close contact with the Hurrians.[80]

In ca. 2010 BC, King Tish-atal brought Ninevah under Hurrian control.[81]

The word "Hurrian" or "Hurri" appears in written history in the 1900's BC, together with information on the Hittites, their cousins. During this era, the Hurrians invaded Syria as far as the Mediterranean coast, and may have been known there as the Horites, the non-Semitic invaders of Palestine and the land of Edom before the Edomites, whose land was

---

[79] Haran was part of the Hurrian Mitanni Empire. (West, 1979)

[80] In the Old Testament, Sarah, the wife of Abraham, was unable to bear a child. According to Hurrian law, Sarah was allowed to give her personal Egyptian slave, Hagar, to Abraham to produce an heir, Ishmael. (Gn 11:30.) Sarah initially allowed Hagar to become a second-class wife to Abraham. The son, Ishmael, however, belonged directly to Sarah. When Sarah wanted Abraham to disinherit Ishmael, Abraham was distressed because this would entail breaking Hurrian law. He therefore sought the guidance of God (clearly not a Hurrian god), who suggested a course of action which Abraham subsequently followed. (West, 1979) These and other Old Testament stories illustrate the influence of Hurrian culture over the lives of the Patriarchs. These laws were inscribed on the Nuzi Tablets.

[81] Cartwright, 2018

on the eastern side of the Jordan River. Excavations at Ugarit or Ras Shamara in Syria, on the coast of the Mediterranean Sea have yielded texts in the Hurrian language.[82]

Sometime around 1900 BC, the Greeks begin referring to the people from both the foothills of the Caucasus and those living in Spain as *Iberians*.

During the 1900's BC, the Hittites first appeared in written history and the historical period of Asia Minor began. The Hittites were a warlike people, descendants of Noah, Ham, Canaan, and Heth, and although it is not known how closely related they were to the Hurrians, they were important in the history of the spread of the Hurrians and are known as the founders of a kingdom which first recorded the history of Asia Minor. Tablets written in the Hittite language yield information on the Hurrian language and reference some Hittite deities which originated as Hurrian deities. The Hittite bas-reliefs in Asia Minor and Syria are Hurrian in style and perhaps in origin (see Figure 7a).

Further, the Hittites are the ancestors of the Etruscans who migrated to Italy ca. 900 BC The Etruscans were skilled metal workers and traders. They were known for their ability to drain land to grow corn and for building irrigation canals.

Tablets found in Hattusa and Ugarit suggest that the Hurrians adopted the Assyrian/Akkadian cuneiform by 2000 BC.

---

[82] About 20,000 cuneiform tablets were discovered in Nuzi. The text concerns Hurrian legal and socio-economic matters.

Also around this time, Hurrian was spoken in southeast Anatolia and the Zagos/Taurus region of north Mesopotamia. The Hurrians were migrating westwards and southwards into these regions between 1900 and 1200 BC.

Hurrian texts dating back to 1800 BC were found in Mari.[83]

---

[83] Modern day Tell Hariri in Syria.

1700 - 1500 BC

From 1750 BC to 1500 BC the Hittite's Old Kingdom was centered in Cappadocia (central Anatolia) and as far as Aleppo (Syria) which is also an area occupied by the Hurrians at one time. This was the time of Jacob in Biblical history, also associated with the Hurrians.

The Hurrians participated in the successful incursions into Egypt during the 1720s BC with the people known as the Hyksos. The Hyksos were thought to be a mixed group of Semites and Hurrians from Palestine, Syria and farther north. According to Biblical history, the Hyksos arrived in Egypt in the 1720s BC.[84]   The Hyksos remained in Egypt until ca. 1560 BC. During their time in Egypt, the Hyksos or the Hurrians are known to have introduced horses and the two-wheeled horse-drawn war chariot to Egypt and Western Asia. By the 1600s BC, the horse and chariot had become common in Egypt.

As a result of the invasions, it is known that the Hurrians were closely allied to the Proto-Aramians (perhaps the forerunners of the land that became known as Mitanni[85])

---

[84] An alternative date for the invasion of the Hyksos is 1680 BC.

[85] Mitanni is referenced in Assyrian, Hittite, and Egyptian texts. Originally they may have been of an Indo-Iranian people. One source suggests that Mitanni was founded by Hurrian King Hirta circa 1500 BC. (Word Heritage Encyclopedia)

and the Assyrians. It is not known what happened to the Hyksos after they left Egypt.

The period from ca. 1800 BC to ca. 1300 BC, appears to be the period of almost five centuries when there is "Silence in the Bible" regarding world history. It also appears that this is the time when Joseph's people were in Egypt before the Exodus.

During the period from 1700 BC to 1500 BC, the Hurrians continued migrating and founded a number of principalities that extended from Carchamish, to Aleppo, to the head waters of the Euphrates, to the vicinity of the Upper Tigris and east of the Tigris in the region of Arrapkha, now known as Kirkuk which had originally been a separate Hurrian kingdom.

Between 1600 and 1430 BC, there was a great deal of antagonism between the Hittites and the Hurrians. The Hurrians overran parts of Asia Minor, Syria, Phoenicia, Jerusalem and the land of Edom. It appears that this period was the golden age of the Hurrians, although subsequently one other group of people who were known to have allied with the Hurrian family also gained political prominence: the Mitanni. The kings of Mitanni eventually joined together the Hurrian principalities.

1500s, 1400s, 1300s BC

In ca. 1500 BC the city of Nawar[86] became an important center of the Kingdom of Mitanni. During this time, a great number of Hurrians were still living in the city and had predominate cultural influence. The city was destroyed by the Assyrians in ca. 1275 BC.

In ca. 1500 BC, Hurrian influence was evident in Syria and the Cilicia region called Kizzuwadna, a Hurrian word.

From 1500 BC to 1240 BC, the Assyrians called the heartland of the Mitanni kingdom, Hanigalbat. This region was predominantly Hurrian in culture.[87]

From about 1500 BC to 1400 BC, the Hurrian/Mitanni Kingdom was considered a world power. Hurrian was the language of this Kingdom.

For the Hittites, this century became an obscure Hittite era during which the Hittites were dominated by the Hurrians.

Fragments of manuscripts (which date to ca. 1500 BC) in cuneiform that record the Epic of Gilgemish have been recovered from the area which was the Hittite capital, Hattusa, now known as Boghaz Keui, in central Anatolia. The languages of the manuscripts include Akkadian, Hittite,

---

[86] The archeological site of Tell Brak.

[87] Cartwright, 2018

and Hurrian. What is particularly interesting is that the Hurrian fragments appear to have been for the use of scribal instruction. This is a cultural marker that indicates the Hurrians were in Hattusa at this time.

For a brief period during the reign of Egyptian Pharoah Thutmoses III, the Mitanni kings were in competition with Egypt over control of Syria.

It is of value to mention at this time, Egyptian Pharaohs of note in Dynasty 18 of the New Kingdom.

Thutmose III (1479-1425 BC) conquered Palestine, Phoenicia, and Syria. Although he reached Carchemish, this city remained under the rule of the Mitanni people. During Thutmose III's reign, *Pharaoh Hatshepsut*, became the first female (1479-1473), to claim co-regency and later the title of Pharaoh of her own standing.

Amenhotep II (1427-1400) followed Thutmose III.
Thutmose IV (1400-1390) then followed. During his reign, friendly relations existed between the Mitanni and the Egyptians.

Amenhotep III (1390 to 1352) whose reign was marked by great prosperity, followed Thutmose IV. Correspondence between Amenhotep III and Hurrian King Tushratta was found among the Amarna Letters[88]. *Amenhotep IV* (1375 to 1349) followed Amentotep III.

---

[88] The Amarna Letters, discovered in 1887, are a group of tablets with cuneiform writing that date back to the fourteenth century BC. They were found at modern day Tell-el-Armana, the ancient short-lived capital, Akhet-Aten, established by Akhenaton.

Amenhotep IV changed his name to *Akhenaton* upon establishing a monotheistic religion that worshiped the one God, Aton. Much scholarly attention has been given to the reign of Akhenaton due to his revolutionary attempt to implement a major cultural shift in Egypt, by removing the pantheon of traditional Egyptian gods and replacing them with a single god. No one knows who or what propelled him to attempt this coup. At the time of his ascension, it is believed that Israelites, who worshiped the one God of Abraham, were dwelling in Egypt. But there is no evidence that they had any direct contact with or influence upon Akhenaton.[89] Despite all of Akhenaton's efforts, his religion and cultural revolution died with him.

Akhenaton's reign was followed briefly by *Smenkhkare* (perhaps a son or daughter), then by *Neferneferuaten* (possibly his wife Nefertiti), then by *Tutankamon*, (d. ca.1340 BC) who was thought to be a son or son-in-law.

Egypt lost control of Syria due to the Hittites around 1400 BC. This date is cited in Biblical history as the apogee of the Hittite civilization in Syria. However, the civilization declined by 1222 BC and came to an end in 1200 BC perhaps because of the Aegean migrations (the Peoples of the Sea) exemplified by the rise of Troy in Anatolia.

From ca. 1475 BC to 1275 BC the kings of the Mitanni continued to flourish in the land of the Hurrians. They adopted Hurrian names and continued to speak Hurrian.

---

[89] The only parallel between the Israelites' and Akhenaton's religion is the similarities between Akhenaton's Hymm to Aton and Psalm 104, both of which celebrate the one God, the creator of the world.

There is evidence that the Hurrians continued to have widespread cultural influence. For instance, fragments of clay tablets dating from ca. 1400 BC, in Ugarit, contain a nearly complete score of music and accompanying text in the Hurrian language using cuneiform. This is thought to be the oldest known musical score.

The Mitanni organized principalities such as the Kingdom of Arrapkha, now known as Kirkuk, which was situated east of the Tigris River not far from Lake Urmia in what is now Iran. This appears to have been the period when the Hurrians, or the Mitanni, conquered the area south of Lake Urmia and as far as the Zagros Mountains also known as Chagha-Khur, close to four hundred miles south of Lake Urmia in Iran. Its capital was Washshukanni, probably located in the Khabur River valley.

Some Hurrian names of the kings of the Mitanni were: Shuttarna I, Shaushtatar, Tushratta, Artatama I, and Shuttarna II.

King Shaushtatar held Aleppo against Thutmose III (1501 to 1447) of Egypt, a feat recorded in a letter found among the official correspondence of the Egyptian kings in the Amarna Letters (1400 BC).

Another Mitannian king, Tushratta, was friendly with Pharaoh Amenhotep III of Egypt, to whom he gave his sister, Gilukhepa (Kilu-Hepa in Hurrian), in marriage[90]. Later, it appears he also gave a daughter, Tadukhipa (Tadu-

---

[90] She became the Pharaoh's secondary wife. Queen Tiye remained the Royal wife.

Heba in Hurrian), to Amenhotep III in marriage. Amenhotep III died shortly thereafter.

The reign of Amenhotep IV followed and Tadukhipa was subsequently given in marriage to him. As mentioned previously, Amenhotep IV changed his name to Akhenaton upon leading a religious revolution in Egypt. His Royal Wife, who is known today as Nefertiti, was then called Neferneferuaten.[91]

Recent studies suggest that Akhenaton's wife, Tadukhipa, may have been his Royal Wife Nefertiti. If this is the case, then Nefertiti would have been a Hurrian princess from Mitanni.[92] and may have been influential in Akhenaton's religious epiphanies.[93] [94]

Sometime after 1275 BC, the Assyrians defeated the Mitanni King Shuttarna II, and the Mittani Kingdom disappeared from history.

Between 1300 and 1200 BC, all Hurrian lands were overrun and became provinces of the Middle Assyrian Empire. Hurrian political power was destroyed. By the end of the Bronze Age, the fate of the Hurrians is unclear. Some suggest that they were absorbed into other cultures of the

---

[91] Her name is translated as "Beautiful are the beauties of Aton, A Beautiful Woman has come."

92 Carroll, 1985

[93] The Mitanni pantheon of Gods included the Orion Sun god, Shimige, who shares attributes with Aton, Akhenaton's god.

[94] Alternative theories exist. One is that Tadukhipa was Kiya, the Mitanni secondary wife of Akhenaton. Kiya disappeared mysteriously after relations between Akhenaton and the Mitanni king became strained.

region.[95]   However, the Hurrian language and elements of their culture continued to influence the Assyrians.

An interesting footnote to history as attested in the Amarna Letters is that apparently during the 1300s BC, only the Egyptian rulers had ready access to gold and Hurrian Kings were known to request gold from the Egyptians as dowries and other exchanges.

---

[95] Cartwright, 2018

Asia Minor 1200 BC

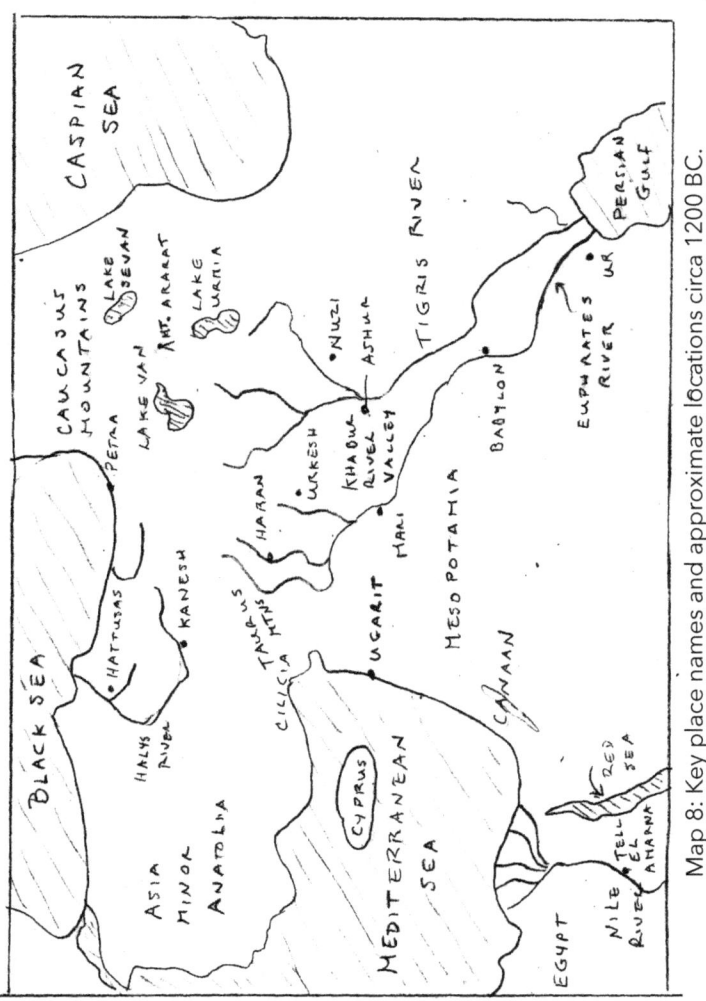

Map 8: Key place names and approximate locations circa 1200 BC.

1300s BC to 612 BC

Some Biblical Considerations

The date of the Exodus has been estimated to have been either 1300 BC or 1250 B. C.

There are several individuals named "Hur" found in the Bible, one of whom occurs in Exodus:17:10-12. "Hur" is mentioned as a companion of Moses and Aaron during a battle with "Amalek". " Hur" was also known in Jewish tradition, as the husband of Miriam, the sister of Moses. This reference may or may not have a connection to the Hurrians mentioned in other sources, inasmuch as the Hurrian language is non-Semitic.[96]

The dates of King Solomon's reign were from 970 BC to 931 BC During his reign, King Solomon had a fleet of Tarshish ships at sea with Hiram's fleet. Tarshish ships were large strong vessels, built for long voyages. Tarshish was also the ancient Tartessus, a Phoenician urban civilization in Southern Spain, the name of which denotes a center for smelting metallic ore. The ships brought gold, silver, ivory, apes, and monkeys to King Solomon's court. As mentioned earlier, King Solomon also imported horses from Cilicia, and chariots from Egypt. He exported them to Hittite and Aramean kings.

---

[96] The origin of the name "Hur" is unknown. However, in Armenian (Aramean), "Hur" means *Fire/Divine Spark*. Related names include: Hor (Egyptian), Haran, Harhaiah, Horite, Hurai, Huri, Hanarai, Nahor, etc.

1200s BC to 600s BC

The Vannic People

During the period from 1270 BC until 612 BC the land between the Caucasus and Lake Van, and from the River Araxes to around Lake Sevan, was known as the land of Uruatri (Assyrian), then later Urartu, and/or as the Kingdom of Van. Its population was basically Hurrian. The Vannic and Hurrian languages appear to be related.

Inscriptions on Assyrian cuneiform tablets contain Vannic records of wars and building operations, particularly hydraulic works and irrigation canals. It should be noted that the building of irrigation canals enabled the highly successful cities of Mesopotamia to flourish.

The Vannic people where known to be skilled in the industrial arts, particularly metallurgy. Their main deities included Tesheba, the Hurrian storm-god Teshub.

The Assyrians called the lands of the people of Urartu, the lands of the Nairi. These lands were located east and north of Lake Van, and were divided into numerous Hurrian principalities. They were subjected to repeated attacks by the Assyrian kings from 860 BC to 733 BC.

In 721, Sargon II of Assyria, after conquering the northern kingdom of Israel, exiled around 30,000 captives (the lost ten tribes of Israel[97]) and dispersed them to distant provinces on the northwestern Iranian Plateau, which was known as the Median Kingdom. Their fate is unknown.[98]

It is believed that a few of the last kings of Urartu were Rusas I, Rusas II, and Rusas III. After the invasion by the Cimmerians, who were from southern Russia, and according to Biblical history, were the descendants of Noah, Japheth and Gomer, the Kingdom of Van was weakened. Thereafter, the Scythians invaded. The Scythians who came originally from directly north of Anatolia, across the Euxine Sea, were the descendants of Noah, Japeth, Gomer and Ripath, the brother of Ashkenaz, and were later known as the Crimean Tartars. After the Scythian invasion. the Medes conquered the country, and the Vannic nation ceased to exist ca. 612 BC.

Meanwhile in ca. 588 BC, King Vishtaspa of Bactria (Persia) was converted by a prophet named Zoroaster to a new religion, Zoroastrianism, one of the earliest monotheistic faiths. Zoraoster henceforth became known as the Prophet of the Persians.

---

[97] The tribes of Reuben, Simeon, Dan, Naphtali, Gad, Asher, Issachar, Zebulun, Manasseh, and Ephraim.

[98] The Book of Tobit (Old Testament) tells of a group of Israelites of the tribe of Naphtali living in the Median Kingdom shortly before 612 BC. Tobit lives in Nineveh (the capital of Assyria) before its fall, however, his friends and kinsmen dwell in various cities of the Medes. Shortly before the fall of Nineveh (612 BC), Tobit, his son and family, migrate to Media.

Iberia 600 BC

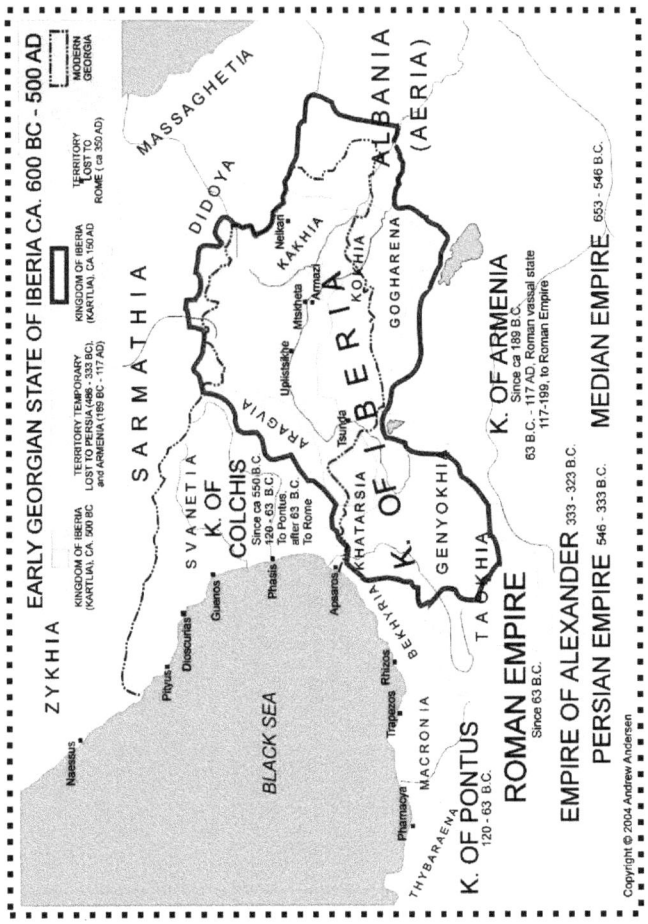

Map 9: The Kingdom of Iberia, ca. 600 BC, in the context of Alexandrian, Persian, Roman, and other land holdings. (Wikipedia Commons [2004 Andrew Anderson:Earlycaucasus655.jpg|Earlycaucasus655]]

300 BC to 30 BC

After the victory of Alexander the Great over the Persian Empire (331 BC), Alexander instituted a cultural fusion of East and West. He settled a large number of Greeks and Macedonians in the Near East and encouraged his men to marry Eastern women. He, himself, married a Persian princess from Bactria, Roxana, and later two other Persian noble women. Hence, Hellenistic culture spread throughout the former Persian Empire. Although this fusion policy did not endure after Alexander's death (323 BC), the spread of Hellenism and the large settlements of Greeks and Macedonians in the region persisted.

A portion of the region thought to be known in antiquity as the Land of the Hurrians, was by this time known as Kartli. Kartli was an economic center located east of another economic power, Colchis.[99]

---

[99]From an examination of several maps which represent the period from pre- 2000 BC to 27 B.C, only two maps, for the periods of l00 BC and 27 BC, show the place called Colchis which is a country on the eastern shore of the Euxine Sea, carved out of the area at the northwestern tip of the Caucasus. However, the people of Colchis and Pontus have been considered to have also been inhabitants of the area known as Iberia, whether this was as early as l263 BC or much later, is under debate. Today, this area is known as the Republic of Georgia, a derivation of Kartli.

Alexander's Successors

200s BC

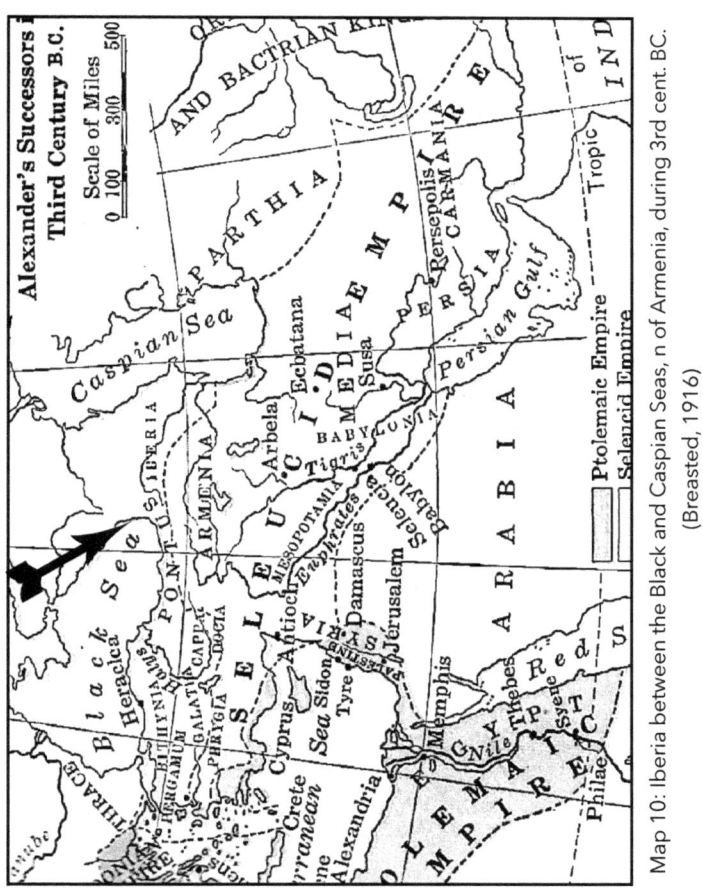

Map 10: Iberia between the Black and Caspian Seas, n of Armenia, during 3rd cent. BC.

(Breasted, 1916)

Pharnavaz became the first king of Kartli in ca. 302 BC. Ancient Greeks who were living in city-states that ringed the Black Sea coast called the lands of Kartli, **Iberia** (see Map 10). The people were henceforth referred to as **Iberians**, and King Pharnavaz is considered the first King of the Iberians.

The lands of the Caucasus (which by this time include the regions of Iberia and Colchis) had long been culturally significant to the Greeks. According to Greek mythology, in 1263 B.C, Jason, the Captain of the Argonauts, was married to the Sorceress Medea, daughter of the King of Colchis. Jason led the Argonauts on an expedition to Colchis to take the Golden Fleece from the King, with the aide of Medea. This suggests the presence of gold in the vicinity of the land of the Hurrians, inasmuch as the fleece from certain sheep were used to sift the gold from other metals or debris, leaving the gold imbedded in the fleece.[100]

The story of Prometheus likewise took place in this region. Prometheus, a son of Zeus, known as a patron to man, stole fire from Hephaestus and gave it to man. As punishment, Prometheus was chained to a high rock in the Caucasus, in perpetuity, to be savagely tortured by an eagle who fed on his liver by day, after which it re-generated at night. Prometheus' cries of pain were renowned. He was eventually saved by Hercules, who in pursuit of his quest for the golden apples, traveled through the Caucasus, found the bound Prometheus, and killed the eagle.

In 65 BC, the Roman General Pompey the Great tried to invade Iberia but was stopped. There is some evidence that

---

[100] Jaramillo

amongst those who were instrumental in defeating Pompey's advance were the Alani (a mixture of Mongolians with Nordic elements). It is not known how long these people had resided in Iberia prior to 65 BC

By 30 BC, Iberia fully accepted protection from Rome.

From this point on, a long period of struggle for control of Iberia among the Kings of Iberia, the successors of the Persians, and the Romans ensued.

100 AD to 888 AD

From 116 to 132 A.D., King Phersman II of Iberia regained some of his power from the Romans. During this same period, the cult of Mithras and Zoroastrianism (from Persia) was commonly practiced in Iberia, despite the influence of the Romans.

By 241 to 272 A.D., this region became less politically Roman and was established as a tributary to the Persian Sasanian state. Zoroastrianism became dominant at this time.

In 298 A.D. Iberia became a vassal state of the Roman Empire. Mirian III[101] was recognized as King of Iberia. His reign lasted until ca. 361 A.D.

---

[101] A contemporary of Constantine the Great.

Through the influence of St. Nino[102], Mirian III became the first Christian King of Iberia and established Christianity as the state religion in 334 A.D.

Mirian III

Figure 10: Sarcophagus of Mirian III (277 - 361 A.D.)
at Samfavro Monastery in Mtskheta, Georgia.
(Wikipedia Commons, by Guro Gabashvili, 2013)

By 363 AD Rome ceded control of Iberia to Persia. Once again, Zoroastrianism was promoted and became the second state religion.

---

[102] St. Nino was a Cappadocian woman who preached Christianity and performed miraculous healings in Eastern Iberia. She acquired great influence over the Iberian monarchy after healing first Queen Nana and later King Mirian III. She is a venerated Orthodox saint whose attribute is a grapevine cross. Her feast day is celebrated on January 14th.

From 363 to 800 AD, there was continual fighting for control over Iberia between the Byzantine Empire and the Persians.

Finally, in 888 A.D. the Iberian and Colchi states were unified and became the United Georgia Monarchy.

This is the end of the chronology for the purpose of attempting to determine the origins of the Eastern Iberians, and why the land known at times as Iberia did not have a permanent name for so many years. The question remains, why was the land ever called Iberia.

According to the Greeks and the Romans, the Celt-Iberian Peninsula was called Iberia because it was named for Eber, the descendant of Noah, Shem, Arpachshad and Shelah, after whom the River Ebro in Spain was named. Is it possible that the Greeks knew from some lost Biblical sources that the area between two rivers, between two seas, between two lakes and at the foothills of a mighty mountain range, was also named for Eber during the time of the descendants of Noah? From Biblical history, we know that an ancestor of Eber, namely Arpachshad, settled the area around Lake Urmia, which was also considered to be part of the land of the Hurrians and it may have been considered a part of Iberia at one time.

Therefore, were the Hurrians the Iberians? Or were the Iberians the Hurrians? Or were the people known as the Iberians sufficiently intermingled with the people known as the Hurrians that during the twenty to twenty-five centuries which followed, there was no difference between them. The name "Hurrian" could be a derivation of another word and it is certainly not too far removed from other names used during that time, for places where the descendants of Noah lived, such as Ur, Urfa, Urautu, Urmia, Erivan, or for the names of his descendants such as Asshur, Uz[103], Hul, etc. The word might also have a special meaning in the ancient languages.

It has been suggested that inasmuch as an open seas navigation culture from the East Mediterranean, called the Cardium culture, existed from as early as the 5th millennium BC, its influence could have extended to the eastern coast of the Celt-Iberian peninsula. These people may have had some relation to the subsequent development of the Celt-Iberian civilization. Were these then the Iberians who traveled from the Caucasus, in Phoenician ships to the Celt-Iberian peninsula since those early days, and did the Greeks know about them since prior to the 6th century BC? They were the people known as the "Iberi" to the Romans. There is evidence that during the Greek Dark Ages, the Greek written language was lost (1100 BC to 700 BC), and thus it is possible that this knowledge may have been carried forward as oral tradition since before 1100 BC.

---

103 In Biblical history, Uz is also a place name somewhere in Edom or Arabia. (Job; 1.1)

Connecting the Dots

To record some observations and a general overall pattern, it would not seem premature to connect some facts:

TO WIT: Copper was known to have been found pre-3500 BC in the area of the Caucasus and the people from that area were known to have developed the art or science of metallurgy. These people became known as travelers, traders, and when necessary, fighters; they were hardy and they knew how to tame and train horses. They were related to many people in Anatolia, and for many years were known as Hurrians. They were certainly known to the Phoenicians, who also were travelers and built their own ships near a place called Tartus on the Mediterranean coast of Phoenicia.

The Phoenicians traveled far away to a land of ore-laden mountains, now known as Spain and called the place Tartessus. They were also related to the Sumerians and to the Urartu who left a record of building operations, particularly hydraulic works and irrigation canals.

CONNECTIONS: the people who developed metallurgy in the Caucasus traveled by Phoenician ships to the area of ore-laden mountains to extract the copper and other metals and to smelt the ore in a land now known as Spain, or the Celt-Iberian Peninsula. These people trained horses and were not averse to traveling and fighting. Before 2000 BC the use of copper was unknown in the rest of Europe; however after that time, this knowledge began to spread from Spain, northward to the rest of Europe.

ERGO: The people from the Caucasus came to Spain circa 2100 BC and having an ancestor by the name of Eber, named a river for him, although at a distance far from their original settlement, because they had good horses and were good travelers and perhaps were searching for other sites for mining; thus the people of this land were thereafter known as Iberians.

Conclusion

To project this information unto the 1500s AD, one can conclude that the Celt-Iberians or the Spaniards, who came to the New World from across the world were also the descendants of the stalwart Eastern Iberians, who were descendants of the ancient Hurrians who had thrived at the foothills of the formidable mountain range known as the Caucasus.

The Celt-Iberians or the Spaniards were good horsemen, and brought horses to the western hemisphere. They were not averse to fighting, as experienced by the Moors, or to traveling to far away places. They brought their knowledge of mining and metallurgy to the western hemisphere. Furthermore, their knowledge of building canals and irrigation systems was essential for the development of agricultural communities in barren land.

It is proposed that the direct descendants of the first families of New Mexico have inherited from their ancient ancestors: personal courage and resilience to move forth and establish new ground when necessary, the tenacity to preserve noble family traditions even in foreign lands, the desire to make use of expertise to improve surroundings, and an attraction to a material culture that includes copper, silver, horses, and easily-transportable goods (including wooden statues of religious significance, see Figures 7a, 11, and 12).

These descendants are a quietly proud people who live their lives with time-honored dignity and faith. ✛

Author's Familial Connections

(Mentioned within *The Brief History of New Mexico*)

Two genealogists, Mrs. Dulemia M. Espinoza and Mr. Eugene E. Jaramillo, who are both cousins of the author, have made it possible to locate and identify many of the names quoted in this monograph. Mrs. Espinoza compiled a thorough genealogical study of family lines on the author's paternal side which go back to Spain as far as 1384, 1380, 1376, and 1372. Mr. Jaramillo has provided information from his wealth of knowledge as well as insight regarding the history, language, and lateral family relationships, in addition to background resources which have been integral to this study.

Some connections of note:

In 1626, Don Pedro Gomez Rico Durán y Chaves was the Commanding General of all Royal Troops in the Kingdom of New Mexico. He had come with Don Juan de Oñate in 1600 with his family. He is a direct ancestor of the author through several lines on both her maternal and paternal sides.

In 1663, Pedro Lucero de Godoy was the Lt. Governor of the Kingdom as well as "Maese de Campo" or Field Marshall of all the military forces in New Mexico. He is the author's direct ancestor through both the author's maternal and paternal lines.

During the two terms, 1722 and 1731, Don Bernardo Bustamente y Tagle was Lt. Governor of New Mexico. He is a direct ancestor of the author through both her maternal and paternal lines.

The author is related to at least ten Governors of New Mexico who served terms beginning from the year 1822, through 1906:

- Francisco Xavier Durán y Chaves – 1822
- Bartolome Baca – 1823
- Manuel Armijo – 1827, 1837, 1845
- Jose Antonio Chaves – 1828
- Francisco Sarracino – 1833
- Mariano Chaves – 1844
- Jose Chaves y Castillo Juan Bautista Vigil y Alarid – 1846
- Donaciano Vigil 1847 (See Illustration 4.)
- Miguel A. Otero 1897 -1906

Some of the Governors are related through both paternal and maternal lines, therefore, they are related in varying degrees.

The Honorable Senator Dennis Chavez in the Congress of the United States since 1930 and a Senator until 1962 is related to the author through both her maternal and paternal lines.

The three Vigil men mentioned in Section VIII as being instrumental in the peaceful turnover of the Department of New Mexico to Gen. Kearny of the United States in 1846 are first cousins four times removed from, and share the same ancestor, Francisco Montes Vigil, (b. ca. 1665) with the author. Francisco was a descendant of Francisco de Vigil de San Martino, (b. ca. 1540), a nobleman of the house of Solar de Vigil in the lugar de Aveno de la Feligresia de San Martino de Asturias, Spain, (an Asturian)[104].

Don Juan Bautista Vigil y Alarid is also related to the author through the Alarid ancestor who was one of the Frenchmen who came to New Mexico and married Spanish women.

The well-known scholar, Fray Angelico Chávez, and the author are related in varying degrees through at least 28 families.

This includes: Alarid, Alvarez del Castillo, Armijo, Durán y Chaves, Baca, de Luna, de Montoya, Martin Serrano, Montes Vigil, Baca, Ortiz, de Vera, Carvajal, Bustamente y Tagle, Pelaez, Gomez Robledo, Romero, Lucero de Godoy, Salazar, Dominguez de Mendoza, Pacheco, Padilla, Fernandez de la Pedrera, Perez de Bustillo, Espinola, de Torres, Tafoya, Vasques De Lara, de Valencia.

One ancestor who bears the intriguing surname "Espinola", could be a descendant of one of the Genoese bankers who financed expeditions to the New World, namely, the famous Spinola family. This is one of those names that requires more research!

---

[104] An aside: Asturias is the only part of Spain which was never conquered by the Moors, and was settled by the Celts and Visigoths.

Further, the County of Valencia, NM, which originally included more than half the state, was named after Blas de Valencia, who came with Oñate in 1598 (See Map 4), was one of the author's ancestors. (Espinosa, 2002)

It should be noted that people from New Mexico who can trace their ancestry to the 1500's and 1600's can probably claim similar multiple ancestry.

In order to round out this narrative, and to come full circle, as it were, there is good reason to believe the claim which has been made in the study by Mrs. Espinosa, which is based on the magnificent magnum opus of Fray Angelico Chávez, that one of our mutual Vigil ancestors is a direct descendant of both Hernan Cortés and Emperor Moctezuma through the Paredes, Montoya, Martin Serrano, Medina, and Vigil lines. An ancestor in this line would be Doña Leónor de Tolosa, the sister of Doña Isabela de Tolosa, the wife of Don Juan de Oñate.

As a sigil or as a seal of authenticity, let it be known that our favorite, distinct, and well-known staple which originated in New Mexico, is spelled **chile** not *chili*. It is unique to us. It is neither Texan nor Mexican!

Our chile comes in two varieties: green and red. When it is used in a beef dish, we call the dish, *chili*. The following recipe, handwritten by Irene Aragon (the author's mother), shows the distinction. The dish called "Chili" uses New Mexican green dried chile.

Joe V. Vigil and Irene C. Aragon, parents of the author, ca 1923.

AN OLD FAMILY RECIPE

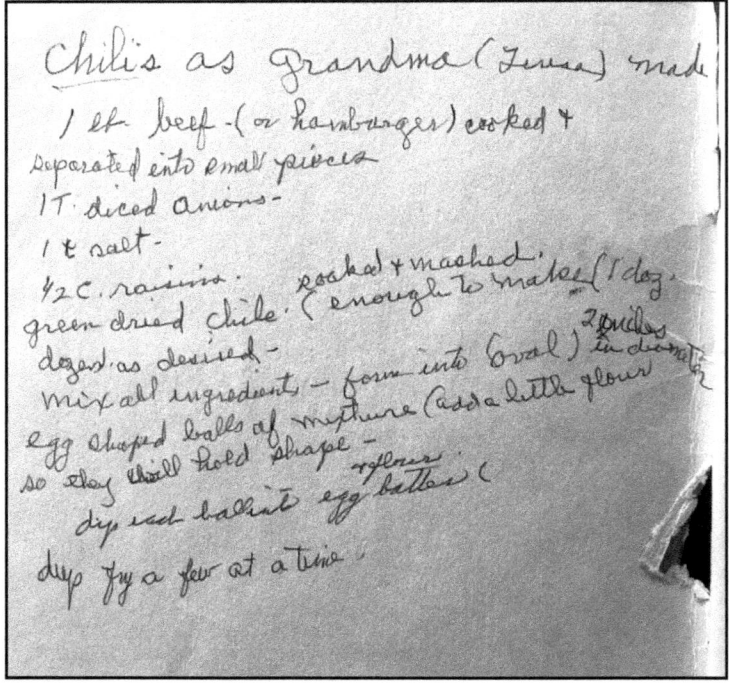

Figure 6: Handwritten recipe by Irene C. Aragon passed down to her from her grandmother, Teresa V. Santistevan Tafoya (1856-1930).

References

Monograph I

Burke, James T. This Miserable Kingdom: The Story of The Spanish Presence in New Mexico. Albuquerque: Our Lady of Fatima Church. 1973.

Chávez, Fray Angelico. Chávez: A Distinctive American Clan of New Mexico. 1989.

Chávez, Fray Angelico. La Conquistadora: The Autobiography of an Ancient Statue. Patterson, New Jersey: St Anthony Guild Press. 1954.

Chávez, Fray Angelico. Origins of New Mexico Families: A Genealogy of the Spanish Colonial Period. Revised Edition. Santa Fe: Museum of New Mexico Press. 1992.

Chávez, Tiro J., Espinosa, Carter M. And Waid. El Rio Abajo. Bishop Publishing Co. 1973.

Espinosa, Dulemia, M. "Ahnentafel Chart for Joseph V. Vigil." Los Lunas, New Mexico: Privately published. May 2002.

Esquivel, J. A. Papers of Merit ... of 17th Century New Mexico Citizens. Privately Published. 1999.

Genders, Ray. Perfume throughout the Ages. New York: Putnam. 1972.

Jaramillo, Eugene. Notes from private letters to Theresa Hooper. Los Lunas, New Mexico. 2006-2014.

Jenkins, Myra Ellen and Schroeder, Albert H. A Brief History of New Mexico. Albuquerque: The University of New Mexico Press. 1974.

Kelly, James C. And Smith, Barbara Clark. Jamestown, Quebec, Santa Fe: Three North American Beginnings. Washington DC: Smithsonian Books. 2007.

Lummis, Charles F. The Spanish Pioneers. 9th Edition. Chicago: A.C. McClurg. 1925.

Reeve, Frank D. New Mexico: A Short, Illustrated History. Denver: Sage Books. 1964.

Simmons, Marc. Coronado's Land: Daily Life in Colonial New Mexico. Albuquerque: University of New Mexico Press. 1991.

Singer, Graciela Gestoso. "Shaushka, the Traveling Goddess." Pontifical Catholic University of Argentina. January 2016. www.researchgate.net/publication/ 322962755.

Twitchell, Ralph Emerson. The Story of the Conquest of Santa Fe and the Building of Fort Marcy. Santa Fe: Historical Society of New Mexico, Vol. 24. 1923.

Figures

Figure 1. Equestrian statue of Juan De Oñate. Oñate Monument Center; Alcalde, NM. By Mario1952, April 30, 2011. https://en.wikipedia.org/wiki/ Equestrian_statue_of_Juan_de_Oñate. (Accessed: August 21, 2021)

Figure 2. Portrait of Captain General Diego de Vargas Zapata Luján Ponce de León y Contreras. Painted by Julio Barrera, date unknown from the collection of the Palace of the Governors, Santa Fe. Source photograph: http://www.ballantinespr.com/ bpr_blogw/2009/03/24/new-mexico-history-museum-don-diego-de-vargas-battle-for-santa-fe/(https://en:wikipedia.org/wiki/ User:Rockero 2006-11-15 01:34.) (Accessed August 21, 2021)

Figure 3. U.S. General Stephen Watts Kearny (Twitchell, 1923, p 5)

Figure 4. Governor Donaciano Vigil (Twitchell, 1923, p 29)

Figure 5. New Mexico Territory coat of arms, 1850. By Henry Mitchell in <u>The State Arms of the Union</u>, Boston: L.Prang & Co. 1876. Restored by Godot13, September 25, 2014. <u>https://</u> <u>c o m m o n s . w i k i m e d i a . o r g / w i k i /</u> <u>File:New Mexico territory coat of</u> arms_(illustrated,_1876).jpg (Accessed: August 21, 2021)

Figure 6: Handwritten recipe by Irene C. Aragon, Valencia, New Mexico.

Maps

Map 1. El Camino Real de Tierra Adentro, (The Royal Road of the Interior Land). By U.S. National Park Service. http:// w w w . n p s . g o v / e l c a , P u b l i c D o m a i n , <u>h t t p s : / /</u> <u>commons.wikimedia.org/w/index.php?curid=35006095</u> (Accessed: July 2021)

Map 2a. NM Villages along the Rio Grande. NM Baptisms, Nuestra enora de la Imnaculada Concepcion de Tome Vol. 1. Compiled by Margaret L. Windham & Evelyn L. Baca. New Mexico Genealogical Society, 1998.

Map 2b. NM Villages along the southern end Rio Grande. NM Baptisms San Miguel de Socorro Church Compiled by Margaret L. Windham and Evelyn Baca. New Mexico Genealogical Society, 1998.

Map 3: 1824. The Department of New Mexico and other territories of the newly independent Mexican Republic. By Giggette, May 2013. https://commons.wikimedia.org/wiki/ File:Mexico_1824_(equirectangular_projection).png

Map 4: Valencia County 1850. By J.A. Curtis 3/10/76. New Mexico 1850 Territorial Census Vol. 1 Valencia County. NM Genealogical Society, Inc. 1991.

Map 5: 1852 New Mexico Territory officially transferred to the United States. By DiltsGD, November 16, 2017. https://en.wikipedia.org/wiki/File:New_Mexico_Territory,_1852.png (Accessed: July 17, 2021)

Monograph II

American Heritage Dictionary, published 1976.

Breasted, James Henry. Ancient Times: A History of the Early World. New York: Ginn and Company. 1916.

Buccellati, Giorgio and Marilyn Kelly. "Urkesh and the Question of the Hurrian Homeland." in The Bulletin of the Georgian National Academy of Sciences, 175, No. 2, 2007. www.academia.edu/40420815/Urkesh_and_the_question_of_the_Hurrian_Homeland (Accessed: June 30, 2021)

Carroll, Warren H. The Founding of Christendom. Volume 1. Virginia: Christendom Press. 1985.

Cartwright, Mark. "The Hurrians." Published on February 15, 2018. www.worldhistory.org/hurrians (Accessed: June 30, 2021)

Castor, Alexis Q. Between the Rivers; The History of Ancient Mesopotamia. Chantilly, VA: The Teaching Company. 2006.

"Caucasian Iberia." Wikipedia, Wikimedia Foundation, https://en.wikipedia.org/wiki/Caucasian_Iberia.

Frahm, Ellery. "Seen Through a Glass Darkly: Re-examining Connections between Mesopotamia and the Caucasus." in Between Syria and the Highlands: Studies in Honor of G. And M. Buccellati. Editors: Stefano Valentini and Guido Guarducci. Rome, Italy: Sanem, Arbor Sapientiae Editore. 2019.

Fournet, Arnaud, and Bomhard, Allan R. "The Indo-European Elements in Hurrian." Charleston: La Garenne Colombes. 2010. www.nostratic.ru/books/(432)bomhard-hurrian.pdf (Accessed: June 30, 2021)

Genders, Roy. <u>Perfume Through the </u>Ages. New York: G. P. Putman & Sons, 1972.

Grovenor, Melville Bell. Editor-in-Chief. <u>Atlas of the World, Third Edition</u>. National Geographic Society. 1970.

Hall, Edward. <u>Wall Chart of History</u>. London: Barnes and Noble. 1995.

Harl, Kenneth W. <u>Origins of Great Civilizations</u>. Chantilly, Va.: The Teaching Company. 2005.

Heritagedaily. "Ancient DNA Research Shines Spotlight on Iberia," <u>www.heritagedaily.com/2019/03/ancient-dna-research-shines-spotlight-on-iberia/122848</u>. March 15, 2009. (Accessed: June 30, 2021)

"Iberian Peninsula." *Wikipedia*, Wikimedia Foundation, <u>https://en.wikipedia.org/wiki/iberian_peninsula</u>.

Jaramillo, Eugene E. Private Papers. 2002.

Langer, W. L. <u>Encyclopedia of World History: Ancient.</u> Cambridge: Harvard Univ., 1948.

Lawler, Andrew. "Who Were the Hurrians?" The Archeological Institute of America, Volume 61, Number 4, July/August 2008. <u>archive.archeology.org/0807/abstracts/html</u>. (Accessed July 2021)

<u>New American Bible, St. Joseph's Edition.</u> New York: Catholic Book Publishing Co., 1970.

Metropolitan Museum of Art, Department of Near Eastern Art. "The Halaf Period (6500-5500 BC)." In Heilbrunn Timeline of Art History, New York: Metropolitan Museum of Art, 2000. <u>www.metmuseum.org/toah/hd/half/hd_half.htm</u>

Ross, Barry L. Professor of Old Testament. "The Patriarchs and Hurrian Legal and Social Customs." Anderson University of Theology, Indiana.

Smith and Peloubet, J.C. <u>Dictionary of the Bible</u>. Winston Co. 1948.

Texier, Charles. <u>Asie mineure description geographique, historique et archeologique des provinces et des villes de la Chersonnése d'Asie</u>, France. 1862. https://en.wikipedia.org/wiki/Šauška (Accessed August 23, 2021)

Toro y Gilbert. <u>Nuevo Pequeno LaRouse.</u> Paris. 195l.

Wells, H.G. The Outline of History. New York: Doubleday & Company, Inc., 1940.

West, Stuart A. "The Nuzi Tablets Reflections on the Patriarchal Narratives." BSP 10:3-4 (Summer-Autumn 1981, p. 74). www.biblia.work/sermons/thenuzi-tablets-reflections-on-the-patriarchal-narratives. (Accessed June 30, 2021)

Figures

Figure 7: Hurrian foundation tablet, circa 2000 BC in the Louvre Museum. By ALFGRN, January 1, 2006. https://www.flickr.com/photos/156915032@N07/47027390354/ (Accessed: August 19, 2021)

Figure 7a: Shaushka by Lushess, 2013, https://en.wikipedia.org/wiki/Šauška (Accessed August 23, 2021. Original from: Texier, Charles. Asie mineure description geographique, historique et archeologique des provinces et des villes de la Chersonnése d'Asie, France. 1862.

Figure 8: Bell Beaker pottery at the Museum for Prehistory and Early History, the State Museum of Berlin, by Einsamer Schutze, June 28, 2011. https://commons.wikimedia.org/wiki/File:Museum_für_Vor-_und_Frühgeschichte_Berlin_026.jpg. (Accessed: August 19, 2021)

Figure 9: Hurrian Lion Peg by the Metropolitan Museum of Art. https://www.metmuseum.org/art/collection/search/329078. (Accessed August 20, 2021)

Figure 10: Sarcophagus of Mirian III at Samfavro Monastery in Mtskheta, Georgia. By Guro Gabashvili, July 8, 2013.

https://commons.wikimedia.org/wiki/
File:King_Mirian_III.jpg (Accessed: August 21, 2021)

Figure 11: La Conquistadora (from Chavez, Fray Angelico. <u>La Conquistadora: The Autobiography of an Ancient Statue.</u> Patterson, New Jersey: St Anthony Guild Press. 1954.)

Figure 12: Our Lady of Peace (from Chavez, Fray Angelico. <u>La Conquistadora: The Autobiography of an Ancient Statue.</u> Patterson, New Jersey: St Anthony Guild Press. 1954.)

Maps

Map 6: A Land Between Two Seas. By T. Hooper and ML Brei, 2021.

Map 7: Middle East 2300 BC. By Jolle at Catalan. December 6. 2004, <u>https://commons.wikimedia.org/wiki/ File:Orientmitja2300aC.png</u> (Accessed: July 24, 2021)

Map 8: Asia Minor 1200 BC. By T. Hooper and ML Brei, 2021.

Map 9: The Kingdom of Iberia, ca. 600 BC. By Andrew Anderson, 15 April 15, 2010. <u>https:// commons.wikimedia.org/wiki/ File:Georgianiberia_andersen565.JPG</u> (Accessed: July 24, 2021)

Map 10: The Three Empires of Alexander's Successors in the Third Century B.C. (from Breasted, James Henry. <u>Ancient Times, History of the Early World</u>. New York: Ginn and Company. 1916)

About the Author

Theresa Vigil Hooper is a direct descendent of the Celt-Iberians who traveled from Spain to New Spain and to the Kingdom of New Mexico as members of the expedition led by Don Juan de Oñate on behalf of the King of Spain in 1598 AD. She was born and raised in New Mexico. She grew up bilingual, speaking both English and 16th-century Castilian Spanish preserved by her family throughout the centuries.

After graduating from the University of New Mexico, she joined the Diplomatic Corps of the U.S. State Department. Because of her unique language skills, she translated original 16th-century Spanish documents and conducted associated research for prominent historians including Dr. Frank D. Reeve (University of New Mexico), Dr. George P. Hammond (UC Berkeley), and Ramon J. Sender. As part of her research at the Bancroft Library, UC Berkeley, her translation of "California's First Book: Reglamento Provicional (1834)" was chosen for publication in 1954.

After marriage, she settled permanently in beautiful Bethesda on the East Coast, raised three children, and enjoyed a successful career in government service. Her passion for research never abated as evidenced by the monographs in this volume.

She died peacefully in 2021, and left her manuscripts in the care of the editor's family to be privately published posthumously.

Theresa Vigil

ca. 1955

1930 - 2021
✝

Post Script

The author, my mother, was convinced that there was a genetic connection between the Ancient Hurrians and her ancestors, the Spanish of the Celt-Iberian Peninsula.

From her dining room table, she scrutinized books, maps, the bible, and other reference material for at least ten years trying to prove her theory. Typically my mother was five years ahead of her time. It is no surprise to me that today, more and more information about the Hurrians is coming to light, consistent with my mother's theories. Ultimately, in my experience, *Mom was always right.*

www.ingramcontent.com/pod-product-compliance
Lightning Source LLC
Chambersburg PA
CBHW051322120626
46547CB00015B/2352